ism is under attack today not only
for its view of language but also for
its view of the literary work, of history, and of the reader. Finally,
Kenneth Burke's discussion of literary form illustrates the impressive
influence of Ransom's theories on
the modern assessment of the nature and function of literature.

*Thomas Daniel Young is Ger-
trude Conaway Vanderbilt Professor of English at Vanderbilt University.*

The New Criticism and After

The
New Criticism
and After

EDITED BY THOMAS DANIEL YOUNG

John Crowe Ransom Memorial Lectures 1975

Delivered at Kenyon College on April 3–5

University Press of Virginia

Charlottesville

THE UNIVERSITY PRESS OF VIRGINIA
Copyright © 1976 by the Rector and Visitors
of the University of Virginia

First published 1976

Library of Congress Cataloging in Publication Data
Main entry under title:

The New criticism and after.

   (John Crowe Ransom memorial lectures; 1975)
    1. Ransom, John Crowe, 1888–1974—Addresses, essays,
lectures.   2. Criticism—Addresses, essays, lectures.
3. Hopkins, Gerard Manley, 1844–1889. The wreck of the
Deutschland.   I. Young, Thomas Daniel, 1919–
II. Series.   PS3535.A635Z79   821'.009   76-6165   ISBN 0-8139-0672-5

Printed in the United States of America

You have heard something muttered in my scorn:
"A little learning addleth this man's wit,
He crieth on our dogmas Counterfeit!
And no man's bubble 'scapeth his sharp thorn;

"Nor he respecteth duly our tall steeple,
But in his pride turning from book to book
Heareth our noise and hardly offereth look,
Nor liveth neighborly with these the people."

"Ego"

True, it is said of our Lady, she ageth.
But see, if you peep shrewdly, she hath not stooped;
Take no thought of her servitors that have drooped,
For we are nothing; and if one talk of death—
Why, the ribs of the earth subsist frail as a breath
If but God wearieth.

"Antique Harvesters"

There must have been debate of soul and body,
The soul storming incontinent with shrew's tongue
Against what natural brilliance body had loved,
Even the green phases though deciduous
Of Earth's zodiac homage to the body.

"To The Scholars of Harvard"

For spin your period out, and draw your breath,
A kinder saeculum begins with Death.
Would you ascend to Heaven and bodiless dwell?
Or take your bodies honorless to Hell?

"The Equilibrists"

Contents

Foreword

In the spring of 1972, before a large audience at Kenyon College John Crowe Ransom made his last public appearance. Standing erect and eager, and wearing a small flower in the lapel of his suit coat, the poet at eighty-four glowed with pride as two undergraduates introduced him and explained that he had agreed to read those of his poems that they had selected as their favorites. He read for over an hour—"Janet Waking," "The Equilibrists," "Piazza Piece," and perhaps a dozen more of his perfectly wrought lyrics. Although his voice quavered occasionally, one mainly heard that inimitable Ransom voice, a subtle combination of formality and humility, dignity and energy, gracefulness and tenderness, anguish and joy that has characterized all his work—as poet, critic, editor, and teacher.

John Ransom's life and work form as coherent a unity as his finest poems. The eloquent and cheerful gentleman who read that night had for the past thirty-three years made his home in this village in central Ohio, miles away from the South where he was born and spent the first half of his life. To imagine him for twenty years in the office of the *Kenyon Review* and in his classrooms, and then for another fifteen in retirement, quietly revising his small collection of lyrics, is to feel sobered and inspired by the knowledge that he went about his work removed from the tumult of our urban literary centers.

Yet Ransom's life was anything but static: serene, perhaps, but always deeply impelled by the desire to revitalize the whole range of humane letters. The story of his achievement is by now a familiar one, a part of our literary history, and any graduate student can rehearse the details of the formalist critical and pedagogical revolution associated with him. In recent years, as some of the essays in this volume testify, many critics have moved beyond the New Criticism, but one cannot avoid the supposition that Ransom would have welcomed this renewed interest in literary theory, as he would have encouraged the ambitious reexaminations of literary and critical assumptions that fill the pages of this book and the pages of the leading journals today.

That was, in any case, our assumption when we chose this manner of commemorating the work of John Crowe Ransom, who died quietly in his home here on July 3, 1974. Each year we would bring to Kenyon writers and critics who continue to explore the fundamental questions about literature: What is it? What is its value? What kinds of questions should we ask about it? How should we study it? How should we teach it?

In this first series of lectures, delivered April 3, 4, and 5, 1975, we tried to strike a balance between assessments of Ransom on the one hand and considerations of new directions in literary study on the other. The diverse interests and positions of the participants seemed to us consistent with the great range of Ransom's own interests; and, as it turned out, a more dynamic and exciting conference could hardly have been imagined. Appropriately one of the high points of the conference was a poetry reading on the evening of the fourth by Robert Lowell, one of Ransom's greatest students. Ransom's daughter, Helen Forman, introduced the poet and recalled Sunday croquet between him and her father in the late 1930s. Lowell's game, she noted, was a constant source of irritation to "Pappy," who played a precise game moved by gentle strokes, while the younger poet indulged himself in exciting long shots, impatient of boundaries. In his reading, Lowell encompassed that dialectic in a way, one feels sure, Ransom would have approved.

For assistance and encouragement we are especially grateful to William G. Caples, President Emeritus of Kenyon College; Philip H. Jordan, the new President; and Robie Macauley, former editor of the *Kenyon Review*. Since the original lectures, published here, we have been fortunate to secure the generous support of the George Gund Foundation, insuring the continuance of the John Crowe Ransom Memorial Lectures for another three years, though the format of these lectures will be altered to make it possible for a single speaker to discuss in detail a particular aspect of literature or criticism each year.

A great deal has happened in the world of letters since John Ransom came to Kenyon, and it is easy to forget how controversial many of his ideas were. We tend to remember Ransom as a highly cultivated gentleman, and he certainly was that; we are less likely to remember the man who chose to write like this in an editorial in the first issue of his new magazine:

One of the pleasantries of Renaissance poets was to assert that verse is immortal. One of the modern evidences is certainly this, that the good verse in English seems to survive imprisonment and bad air, in the unlovely context of schoolbooks, and the rack and screw, in the authorized distortions of pedants, who are placed over the courses in literature by the Colleges. I should prefer not to estimate the percentage of pedants in the total number of professors; it is particularly high within the "Departments of English."

Bold and spirited yet elegant and decorous, Ransom was a complex man, but above all he was a person of deep humanity and vision. The John Crowe Ransom Memorial Lectures are meant to honor the man who, as Hugh Kenner has said, "exerted more influence on humane learning in America than possibly anyone else in this century."

GALBRAITH M. CRUMP
WILLIAM F. KLEIN
RONALD A. SHARP

Gambier, Ohio

December 15, 1975

Acknowledgments

The letters of John Crowe Ransom are quoted by permission of Robb Reavill Ransom. Excerpts from "Survey of Literature," "Captain Carpenter," "Antique Harvesters," "To the Scholars of Harvard," and "The Equilibrists," from John Crowe Ransom, *Selected Poems*, 3d ed. revised and enlarged, © 1969 by Alfred A. Knopf, Inc., are quoted by permission of the publisher. Excerpts from "That Nature Is a Heraclitean Fire" and "The Wreck of the Deutschland," from *The Poems of Gerard Manley Hopkins*, 4th ed., revised and enlarged, © 1967 by Oxford University Press, are quoted by permission of the publisher.

Introduction

ALMOST NO ONE who is aware of the main currents in British and American literature in the period between the two world wars would doubt that John Crowe Ransom was one of the most influential men of his generation. In a very small body of poetry—the last edition of his *Selected Poems* (1969) has only eighty titles—he demonstrated his ability to serve as effective spokesman for his age. Few other poets of this century have been able to reflect with greater accuracy and precision the modern sensibility, to represent the inexhaustible ambiguities, the paradoxes and tensions, the dichotomies and ironies which characterize the life of modern man. A few of these nearly flawless lyrics will be read as long as poetry endures. But Ransom's reputation today is not based upon his poetry alone; he is remembered by many readers for his eloquently written essays in which he castigates his fellow men for deifying reason, worshipping science and rejecting the God of old, for allowing themselves to become enslaved to an ever-expanding industrial system that has dehumanized their lives. Some undoubtedly regard as Ransom's primary contribution to American letters his theoretical studies of the nature and function of poetry. His explorations into the cognitive functions of poetry—as altered, expanded, and retailed by his students and followers and their students and followers—form persuasive arguments for the importance of the arts. He insisted that poetry allows us to know the world in all its rich materiality, which science with its emphasis on abstraction would destroy. Only through poetry may we recover "the denser and more refractory original world which we know loosely through our perceptions and memories."

If nothing except published work is considered, one may conclude that Ransom's literary career can be divided into three separate periods. In the first, from about 1917 until 1925 or '26, he was a poet, writing during this period almost all of his important poetry—that included in *Poems about God* (1919), *Chills and Fever* (1924), and *Two Gentlemen in Bonds* (1927). Then, with his career as publishing poet behind him, he turned to other interests. His conviction that modern man needed an inscrutable God, one that can neither be comprehended by reason nor explained by scientific fact, led him to publish *God without Thunder* (1930). His investigations of man's relationships with God, with nature, and with his fellow man drew him into his Agrarian period, in which he contributed essays to *I'll Take My Stand* (1930) and *Who Owns America?* (1936). During these ten years—from 1927 to 1936—much of Ransom's creative energy was expended in producing essays under such titles as "The South Defends Its Heritage," "Modern with the Southern Accent," and "What Does the South Want?"—essays in which he joined his fellow Agrarians in protesting against further industrialization of the South and urging the southerner to defend his Agrarian tradition so that he would not become a mere automaton in an industrial society with an inordinate emphasis on immediate material profit. Again, it would seem, the pattern recurred. Having devoted his best efforts for a time to religion, economics, and politics, his interest in those fields waned, and he focused his now fully developed analytical powers on other subjects. He returned to literature, but this time his concern was literary theory, and the remainder of his career was devoted almost exclusively to speculations on the nature and function of poetry.

This view, it would appear, is too simplistic, for it fails to take into consideration the most conspicuous and the most persistent quality of Ransom's temperament. Although in different periods he shifted his attention from one area to another, his principal concerns remained unchanged. A man of considerable logical powers, Ransom took pride in his logical consistency. "Logic," as Allen Tate has observed, "was the mode of his thought and sensibility." His literary career can best be understood, therefore, as an attempt to bring all his apprehensions and interests under one rational system. Beginning with definite assumptions, which he supported with both passion and conviction, he was able to bring order and shape to some of his powerful emotional experiences through logical argument. In much of his best poetry, as Louis D. Rubin, Jr., points out, he articulated man's proper position in the universe, and the theoretical discussions in *God without Thunder* and the Agrarian essays gave him the opportunity to systematize those conclusions. A proposed book on aesthetics—in which Ransom hoped to demonstrate that man can know the concrete particularity of the world's body only through dreams, fancies, religion, morals or art—became *God without Thunder*, in which he contends that the "God of the Jews has been whittled down by science." Modern man denies myth and is interested only in facts which have been registered on one or more of the five senses of an honest and reliable observer. This worship of science not only has destroyed the inscrutable, contingent, mysterious God of the Old Testament, but it has also given man a false sense of superiority over nature, a conviction that nature can and should be harnessed and used for his benefit. This view of nature leads directly into a principal tenet of his Agrarian writing: "Nature industrialized, transformed into cities and artificial habitations, manufactured into commodities, is no longer nature but a highly simplified picture of nature."

Ransom's support of the Agrarian community, Rubin argues convincingly, was the result of his conviction that in it both religion and art could flourish, in it the desire to control and possess the natural object had been "domesticated and controlled" through ritual, ceremony, and contemplation. "Art, religion, agriculture, and the South," Rubin points out, "are made into one coherent artistic image" in "Antique Harvesters," a poem published five years before Ransom became involved in a systematic defense of religious myth and the Agrarian tradition. In this poem the attitudes and convictions he would express in *God without Thunder* and the Agrarian essays had already been presented through images, and Ransom's career as poet had nearly ended. Now he set about the business of giving order and system to these deeply felt convictions through dialectic and argumentation. He defended, in a series of logically developed essays, conclusions which he had reached almost instinctively and had not given the intellectual support that his kind of sensibility demanded. He came to defend an Agrarian society because he was convinced that only in that kind of political and social order could the arts flourish. His forays into the field of economics soon persuaded him that Agrarianism was an impractical approach to the region's problems; therefore he retreated from Agrarianism as he had entered it, through aesthetics.

If modern man must live in an industrial society enamored with material gain, what is to happen to the arts and the artists? In the early 1950s, after his formal announcement in 1945 that Agrarianism was no longer a major concern of his, Ransom responded to this question with a variation of an observation that he had made almost twenty years earlier. In "Poets without Laurels" (1935) he had pointed out that "poetry as a living art has lost its public support," for although a "small company of adept readers" might enjoy modern verse, the "general public detests" it. The poet must realize, therefore, that he can expect few laurels from the public at large. There is, he pointed out nearly twenty years later, a smaller but "much more tolerant and humane" order to which we can belong—that is, to the community of letters. "The role of literature," he remarked in "The Communities of Letters" (1952), "is partly, and in recent times it seems often to be chiefly, to make public not the area of experience which is already public, where the focus of attention is on the constitution of the formal society and the obedience of its members to the code, but that area of experience which is most private, and never comes to public judgment." There are many communities of letters, for the public of each important writer forms a separate one. The kind of knowledge which only the poet can offer and which can only be apprehended aesthetically cannot be translated literally into the formal society and must be passed among the many communities of letters.

It may be argued, then, that Ransom never abandoned literary criticism, that aesthetic speculation was the soil from which the other activities—the poetry, *God without Thunder,* and the Agrarianism essays—got their sustenance. In February 1914 he outlined in a letter to his father a "theory of poetics" which he elaborated and expanded for the next half century. This letter includes a rudimentary statement of critical positions that he would restate for the remainder of his career. Although poetry is not an important medium of instruction, it is a unique means of cognition. It provides an order of knowledge that is "ontologically distinct" because from it we can learn "what we have arranged that we cannot know otherwise." In many later essays he attempted to define that "precious object," the poem, through which this order of knowledge is transmitted, that mode of expression composed of an "ostensible argument" which can be rendered in prose and a "tissue of meaning" which cannot. The poet wants always to restore the world's body, to infuse into the consciousness of his reader that knowledge which only art can provide, an awareness of the object for its own sake.

Throughout his career John Crowe Ransom maintained that human experience can be fully realized only through art, and this conviction underlies all his creative endeavors. Ransom's poetry delineates with great force and clarity the plight of man: his dual nature and the tragedy that always follows the failure to recognize this fact—his ability to function in the modern world depending upon his being able to hold in equilibrium two contradictory ideas. Since his poems mirror the modern sensibility, they are an invaluable and almost inexhaustible source of knowledge because from them the contemporary reader can reconstitute the common actuals of his experience. If the poet is to perform this unique function, Ransom was convinced, he must be a member of a society that permits the ceremonies of poetry and provides a sympathetic audience to perceive the distinct order of knowledge that it contains. For a time he thought an Agrarian society would provide the kind of leisurely existence in which poetry could be created and meditated. Later, when his logical analyses of that social order convinced him that such a system was not feasible in the twentieth century, he did not abandon his belief in the value of poetry as a means of cognition. He altered his conception of the nature of the audience in which the poet could be heard. Since the artist cannot expect either to form or to recall a formal society sympathetic to the arts, he must be content with the reaction that his creations produce among the "few choicer spirits here and there who can respond to an order of fiction advanced either in its boldness or in its subtlety." If he is convinced of the limitations placed upon the artist because of the restrictions imposed upon him by an alien social order, he is nonetheless certain of the importance of artistic expression. He still insists that "art is the freest and fullest and most sympathetic image of the human experience—none of the adjectives can be spared." After his repudiation of Agrarianism, Ransom devoted much of his time to defining the unusual nature of the poetic structure, and in recounting the significance of its cognitive function by contrasting its aims and purposes with those of science.

Ransom's "Criticism, Inc." (1937) has often been cited as the essay that ushered in the era of formal criticism, an approach to literary study that emphasized the kind of insights that may be derived only from an intensive study of the literary work itself. In that essay and in others written before and since, he insisted that if the poem is to reveal its unique order of knowledge that it must be read as poem and not as something else. The year following the publication of this essay, *Understanding Poetry*, edited by Cleanth Brooks and Robert Penn Warren, carried into the classroom the critical approach that Ransom had called for. To attempt an estimate of the effect that volume and its many imitators have had upon the way poetry is taught today would be virtually impossible. For this reason Hugh Kenner can say that in spite of the fact that hardly anyone bought the books Ransom wrote, his "unusual powers were aided by an historical opportunity" and no one "has had more effect on the way the subtler operations of language are

apprehended in the country in this century." In the teaching
Ransom did, and in that done by his students and followers and by
their students and followers, readers were instructed in how to
value the poem for its own sake, how to avoid the biographical
fallacy, how to recognize the strategy of using the poem to
illustrate some historical process, how to employ the poem as a
means of realizing the world. Perhaps, Kenner suggests, Ransom's
art had less to do with criticism itself than it did with the study of
literature. At any rate the approach to literature he practiced himself and fostered in others returned the study of poetry to the
"central American intellectual concern which is language."

There seem to be few New Critics around today, but this
concern for language, "the means of representation in literature,"
is masterfully demonstrated in J. Hillis Miller's illuminating study
"The Linguistic Moment in 'The Wreck of the Deutschland,' " in
which he attempts "to honor the example of John Crowe Ransom's
criticism." Although Miller shares Ransom's interest in exploring
exactly how language functions in the poem, their emphases differ.
Whereas Ransom was primarily concerned with indicating how the
uses of language in the structure of a poem vary from those in its
texture, or why the scientific symbol is not the same as the poetic
icon, Miller concentrates upon the "moment when language as
such ... becomes a matter to be interrogated, explored,
thematized in itself." From such questioning, and not through discussions of ethical or metaphysical themes, he hopes to
demonstrate how literature may be "distinguished from other uses
of language." Formal criticism, as Ralph Cohen points out, is
under attack today not only for its view of language but also for its
"view of the literary work ..., of history, and of the reader."
Many critics today—one of whom is Geoffrey Hartman—believe
"explication-centered criticism" is merely "preparatory to the
study of poetry." Interpretation must be related to the poet's
understanding of experience, including the "poet's understanding
of earlier poets." Others, among them Harold Bloom, argue that
no poem is an autonomous object; therefore it should be read as
"its poet's deliberate misinterpretation, *as a poet*, of a precursor
poem or of poetry in general." These efforts to expand the meaning
of interpretation have been complemented in the work of Stanley
Fish, who insists that meaning must be considered in terms of the
informed reader. What a poem by Pope means to a reader with extensive formal study in eighteenth-century literature is likely to

differ a great deal from what it means to a reader without this study.

The formalist critic regard the explication of a specific poem as an acceptable interpretation because it identifies the individual character of the poetic structure under consideration. But "explicative interpretation" is unsatisfactory to the contemporary critic whose views are governed by the "premises that language is acculturated and that literary work does not have an objective life aside from interpreters." To these critics—as well as to those who "view the literary work as event," or to those who emphasize the "historicity of literary language and form or the nature of the reader's response"—explication is not enough.

In one of his best-known essays Ransom argues that because criticism "must become more scientific or precise and systematic" it should be "seriously taken in hand by professionals." There is little evidence that the "trained performers," as he referred to his fellow critics, have taken seriously his suggestion that they form a corporate body—a "Criticism, Inc." or "Criticism, Ltd."—so that they could discharge more effectively their "proper business of interpreting literature." Another of his recommendations, it would seem, however, has had a more favorable reception. University professors of literature have taken "critical activity in hand." In the two decades since "Criticism, Inc." was published, the pedagogue has become critical as well as learned. He not only permits his students "to study literature and not merely about literature," but in his classroom and through essay and book, as the present collection illustrates, he demonstrates how this important activity is carried on by the professional. That his own example might have encouraged a development in which so much effort and expertise would be devoted to the understanding and communication of literature must have been most gratifying to the man whom the essays that follow propose to honor.

THOMAS DANIEL YOUNG

The New Criticism and After

A Critic Almost Anonymous
John Crowe Ransom Goes North

Louis D. Rubin, Jr.

IN THE LATE MONTHS of the year 1929, on the eve of the Great
Depression, a group of poets and teachers at Vanderbilt University
who were shortly to become known as Agrarians were readying
plans for their symposium *I'll Take My Stand: The South and the
Agrarian Tradition.* In this book they would warn against the dehu-
manizing consequences of the further industrialization of the
South, call upon southerners to safeguard their agricultural tradition, and urge a determined resistance to industrial development
and commercial progress. One of them, Allen Tate, in Paris,
thought it best to warn another, Donald Davidson, in Nashville,
that "we exhibit two sorts of minds. You and Andrew [Lytle] seem
to constitute one sort—the belief in the eventual success, in the
practical sense, of the movement. The other mind is that of
Ransom, Warren, and myself. I gather that Ransom agrees with me
that the issue on the plan of action is uncertain."[1] Tate went on to
assure Davidson in this letter of November 1929 that it didn't matter that he was skeptical of practical success, and that there was
enough of value to satisfy him in the affirmation, "in all its consequences, including action, of value."

For once at least Tate was wrong about John Ransom, I think.
Ransom may have come to Agrarianism by way of aesthetics and
philosophy, but once he got there he viewed it, however
guardedly, as a practical matter, and he hoped to have a direct im-
pact upon the South and, through the South, upon the nation. For
Ransom it was a commitment to action, and one that he fulfilled
for some years before giving it up. From the late 1920s almost until
he came to Kenyon College in the fall of 1937, he was an Agrarian,
and he meant it.

Whatever private reservations John Ransom might have
entertained concerning the practicality of Agrarianism in the years
while *I'll Take My Stand* was being assembled, once the book was
out he plunged into a thoroughgoing involvement in the enterprise

---

[1] *The Literary Correspondence of Donald Davidson and Allen Tate,* ed. John
Tyree Fain and Thomas Daniel Young (Athens: University of Georgia Press, 1974),
p. 241. Subsequent letters are shown by date only.

as a viable, expedient program for the South. It was Ransom who debated Stringfellow Barr before an audience of several thousand persons in Richmond in late 1930. Twice more in the succeeding months he defended the Agrarian cause in public debate, and since the chief weapon his opponents used against the movement was the claim that it was visionary and impractical, Ransom concentrated upon the attempt to demonstrate its utility.

To do this, he was drawn into economics to a much greater extent than ever before in his career, and he responded by undertaking a determined study of farming, politics, and finance. In 1931–1932 he received a Guggenheim fellowship and went to England with the intention of writing a book to be entitled *Land!*, in which he would set forth the case for agrarian self-sufficiency for America. The manuscript was rejected by various publishers, however, and Ransom concluded that he did not really know enough about advanced economics to be able to write authoritatively on the subject. But his interest in what the South should do with its economy and its life did not wane as yet; he published a number of articles, reviews, and essays which focus upon that concern. The titles alone are indicative of how seriously he viewed the problem: "The State and the Land," "Land! An Answer to the Unemployment Problem," "Happy Farmers," "A Capital for the New Deal," "Sociology and the Black Belt," "What Does the South Want?," and "The South Is a Bulwark."

During those years Ransom published almost no poetry; his career as a poet had pretty much come to an end with the late 1920s. There is no government regulation, as Ransom once observed wryly, that requires a man to continue to write poetry all his life; and it may be that his forsaking the muse while still in his middle-forties was a conscious decision. Yet one is not disposed to leave the matter there. Why did this highly accomplished poet, who once regularly published poetry and who remained, for the rest of his long life, profoundly committed to poetry and poetics, cease almost overnight to write poems? What did it have to do with his Agrarian interests? Finally, why, when he ceased to write about Agrarianism and the South, did he do so with such abruptness, and feel it obligatory to repudiate his previous positions?

John Ransom was a man of great logical powers who prided himself upon logical consistency. But the logic was not open-ended; he started with some formidable assumptions, to which he was drawn by powerful emotions; and dialectic and argumentation for Ransom were a way of disciplining and ordering a passionate emotional experience. If the conclusions toward which his thinking led him were sometimes oddly logical and abstract, the emotional and psychological need that those conclusions played in ordering his life was deeply felt and passionately apprehended. Logic systematized his emotions; he did not reason himself into Agrarianism, as Frank Owsley said, so much as formulate a rational system, which involved a program, that would systematize and objectify loyalties and spiritual necessities which were strongly felt. In poems such as "Antique Harvesters," "Amphibious Crocodile," "Conrad in Twilight," and "Armageddon," written before Agrarianism had emerged from his thinking as a programmatic system, Ransom had already articulated his feelings about man's (including his own) proper condition in the universe. The ensuing theory, in *God without Thunder: An Unorthodox Defense of Orthodoxy* and in the essay "Reconstructed but Unregenerate," was his way of systematizing his conclusions. This was very necessary to Ransom; he was not a man for whom an implicit, blurred intellectual situation was acceptable. He had no taste for leaving things on the surface; he demanded exploration and explication, and he was not content until or unless his apprehensions were linked up in an ordered and rational system.

Yet here we are faced with a paradox. Philosophically Ransom was not only a dualist, but his philosophy, his aesthetics, and his poetics alike were predicated upon the inadequacy of intellectual formulations and philosophical systems—and the falsification of reality that resulted when they were imposed upon the complexity of human experience. The most fiercely opprobrious term that he could apply to any intellectual or aesthetic position was to say that it was Platonic. In Ransom's aesthetics Platonism is as villainous a force as Industrialism is in his economics. He even wrote a poem about it, entitled "Survey of Literature," which begins: "In all the good Greek of Plato / I lack my roastbeef and potato."

God without Thunder, which started out as a book on aesthetics, had developed the argument that western society, in turning to the Platonic worship of the Logos rather than the Old Testament God of awe and mystery, had deified reason and opened the way to the worship of science, thus losing the sense of wonder and dependence of a God who can be feared and loved. The absence of such supernatural authority as restraint had made possible the limitless exploitation of nature in terms of its material usefulness, through industrialism which is the economic method of applied science. In devouring nature, predatory industrialism also used men, degrading and brutalizing labor. The modern city was industrialism incarnate; shielding its inhabitants from any sense of the infinitude and mystery of nature, it gave men the illusion of mastery over nature, and at the same time forced them into the status of production units designed to make and consume material goods. They were thus prisoners of an everexpanding, ever-devouring industrial system that dehumanized their lives and pressed them into joyless labor on behalf of an insatiable big-business establishment. Under such a continuously driving industrial dispensation, neither religion nor art is possible, since both depend upon the sense of reality as something ultimately mysterious. Without ritual and contemplation there can be only naked human aggression.

So the Agrarian community, for Ransom, was that in which, because the savage industrial drive toward mastery over nature has not been permitted to destroy the human sense of mystery and finiteness in the face of nature, religion and art *are* possible. Aggression, the desire for possession, has been halted—or rather, domesticated and controlled—through ritual and contemplation.

All these images were fused in "Antique Harvesters," written in 1924, in which the harvesters till the earth and gather the bronze treasure for the Lady, while the hunters, "keepers of a rite," ride by in pursuit of "the fox, lovely ritualist." Art, religion, agriculture, and the South are made into one coherent artistic image. In the ensuing five years he reasoned out the theory that the poem incorporated.

The Agrarian society therefore is the place for poets. The Agrarian South is again and again presented in Ransom's essay *I'll Take My Stand* as a work of art. "The South took life easy, which is itself a tolerably comprehensive art," the author declares in summation. He defines the true farmer as one who "identifies himself with a spot of ground . . . would till it not too hurriedly and not too mechanically to observe in it the contingency and the infinitude of nature; and so his life acquires its philosophical and even its cosmic consciousness." Ransom thus advocates "the clean-cut policy that the rural life of America must be defended, and the world made safe for the farmers." It goes without saying that this situation is ideal for a poet, too. As Ransom declares in the "Statement of Principles," "art depends, in general, like religion, on a right attitude to nature; *and in particular on a free and disinterested observation of nature that occurs only in leisure*" (italics mine).[2] But not only

[2]Twelve Southerners, *I'll Take My Stand: The South and the Agrarian Tradition* (1930; rpt. New York: Harper & Row, Harper Torchbooks, 1962), pp. xix–27.

for the farmers. For if poetry depends upon the "right attitude to nature," the free and disinterested observation that comes only with a leisure denied to an industrialized society, then to make the world safe for farmers is also to make the world safe for poets—in which category may be numbered, among others, John Crowe Ransom.

Ransom saw industrialism and urban society as inimical to the nature of poetry, and agrarianism and rural society as essential to it; and if we search out the delineation of his ideal agrarian society, it is obvious that he viewed himself, in no exclusive sense, as its poet. If we examine the motifs and imagery of the poetry he wrote, he had every right to make this identification. He also saw his poetry, and poetry in general, as drawing upon the same impulses and assumptions as religion, involving a sense of mystery and awe, the product of ritual and contemplation. For him poetry is inimical to the aggression and exploitation of an industrial society. We might recall that, back in his young manhood, he had written to his clergyman father in the spring of 1913 to identify the artist with the moralist: "He is interested in humanity, its vivid passions, its subtle refinements, its slow fires; he communicates the fascination of the study and thereby becomes a moral preceptor."

Therefore, when Ransom mounted his campaign for Agrarianism in the late 1920s and the early 1930s, he was also waging a campaign for poetry and religion, and for a rigorously logical mind like his the congruence of the activities was not only explicit but essential. He wasn't, from his standpoint, engaged in the one activity instead of, or in addition to, others; they were part and parcel of the same enterprise, and what was involved in the early 1930s was an emphasis upon the economic aspect of a single human predicament.

When the critics of Agrarianism began taking the approach as they customarily did, that it was a visionary, impractical enterprise which failed to take account of the actual needs of the southern agricultural situation, Ransom's response was predictable: he undertook an intensive study of economics in order to demonstrate the utility of Agrarianism, and he wrote articles based on his study. Of all the charges that might have been brought against the enterprise, surely the notion of its being a utopian, theoretical scheme, an idea that failed to take account of the economic actualities, must have irked him most. For if the charge were true, that would make it nothing less than a Platonic affair, an abstract design: one which imposes its holder's heart's desire upon recalcitrant human experience, to shape it to his liking through an act of the naked will. Clearly this would not do: Agrarianism *had* to be practical, it had to fit the human, economic facts and not ignore them, and Ransom was not about to countenance the possibility that it didn't. If Agrarianism, like the good Greek of Plato, left out the roast beef and potato of the agricultural situation, then it was nothing that a poet ought to be engaged in promoting.

It was in the period 1931–1932, when Ransom was in England, that he wrote a long two-part essay entitled "A Poem Nearly Anonymous," which was published in the *American Review*. Later the essay appeared under that title for the first part and "Forms and Citizens" for the second in *The World's Body*.[3] This was Ransom's first major essay on poetics. *God without Thunder* had started as a work on aesthetics, to be entitled "The Third Moment," but its author had moved into theology and Agrarianism. The new essay was a brilliant piece of theorizing, in which Ransom used Milton and "Lycidas" to develop a complex theory of poetics. He followed it with "Poetry: A Note on Ontology" (1934), one of the seminal critical writings on the nature of poetry for the next several decades; no discussion of twentieth-century poetic theory can omit a consideration of this essay. In 1935 Ransom produced three more major essays on poetry and aesthetics—"Poets without Laurels," "The Cathartic Principle," and "The Mimetic Principle." These pieces established him as one of the important literary thinkers of his time. Until they appeared his reputation had been that of a distinguished lyric poet who had also produced some interesting but narrowly focused prose having to do with regionalism and traditionalism. Now he was a major critical theorist whose views were discussed on two continents.

In 1937 came a crisis in Ransom's career.[4] He was approached by the new president of Kenyon College and invited to come there as professor of poetry. Having spent all but eight years of his life since 1903 at Vanderbilt University, the notion of seriously considering a permanent move elsewhere came as a shock. But he was weary of the heavy burden of committee work at Vanderbilt, and the Kenyon salary was decidedly better than his Vanderbilt stipend of just under four thousand dollars. When it became evident that

[3] *The World's Body* (New York: Scribners, 1938). All quotations from "A Poem Nearly Anonymous" and "Forms and Citizens" are taken from this source.

[4] For a full discussion of this episode, see Thomas Daniel Young, "In His Own Country," *Southern Review*, NS 8 (1972), 572–93.

Ransom was seriously considering leaving, Tate wrote an open letter to Chancellor James C. Kirkland of Vanderbilt, sending a copy to the Nashville *Tennessean,* in which he denounced Vanderbilt's failure to appreciate the international distinction that Ransom and his activities had brought to it.

The question of Ransom's status quickly became a cause célèbre. *Time* magazine sent a reporter to investigate. The position of Kirkland and of Edwin Mims, chairman of the Vanderbilt English department, was that Vanderbilt could not give Ransom a higher salary than others at the same rank. Donald Davidson was enraged; in a face-to-face confrontation with Mims he asserted himself as he had never been known to do. The newspapers were full of articles describing the situation. The Vanderbilt board of trust was approached. A testimonial dinner was organized for Ransom. Distinguished literary figures from America and Europe sent telegrams.

Apparently Kirkland did finally consent to place the matter before the board of trust, with the understanding that a five-hundred-dollar yearly increment would be forthcoming from the alumni association to supplement Ransom's $4200 salary, through an anonymous gift—if Edwin Mims wished it done. Mims, however, would not agree. He was not willing for Kirkland to propose special arrangements for Ransom, and he "never thought that Vanderbilt should match the Kenyon College offer." So no action was taken, Ransom announced his resignation at the testimonial dinner, and Edwin Mims, who had built his Vanderbilt English department into one of international prominence, had now consented to its being wrecked. Only Donald Davidson, of all those who had made the *Fugitive* into the magazine it was and had then unloosed the Agrarian jehad, was left. That fall Ransom began his tenure at Kenyon College.

Why did Ransom decide to leave Vanderbilt? It could not have been money, since the sum finally authorized by Vanderbilt, though never actually offered, was, as Thomas Daniel Young says, certainly competitive. Ransom had become tired of his work on curriculum revision. To a newspaper reporter in Boulder, Colorado, he declared that "I think in a smaller college I'll have more time for writing. In a large university there are so many demands upon a person's time—committees and curriculum reform and paper work and all of that." He liked the idea of being professor of poetry rather than professor of English, he said. I imagine that he was also favorably impressed with Gordon Keith Chalmers, the new Kenyon president, and that he had some encouragement that

such developments as the *Kenyon Review* and the Kenyon School
of English were to be possible.

Yet more than this was involved in John Ransom's decision to
leave Vanderbilt and Nashville. It had more than a little to do with
Agrarianism or, rather, with Ransom's loss of interest in it. Ransom
wanted to leave Nashville. He had come to feel that as long as he
remained there he would be caught up in and identified with Agrarianism, and by 1937 he had had just about all the Agrarianism he
wanted. He wanted to get back to poetry—if not to the writing of
it, then at least to writing about it.

I propose now to look at "A Poem Nearly Anonymous" and its
sequel, "Forms and Citizens," which he wrote while the Agrarian
interest was still apparently in full swing, and which turned out to
be the first statement of the new preoccupation with poetry and
poetics that would come to the forefront in the middle 1930s and
thereafter become his chief attention for the remainder of his life.

The poem nearly anonymous is "Lycidas," which Ransom
describes as a work of "an apprentice of nearly thirty, who was still
purifying his taste upon an astonishingly arduous diet of literary
exercises." Throughout most of the poem the personality and the
direct autobiographical concerns of Milton the man are suppressed
in favor of those of Milton the poet. "Milton set out to write a
poem mourning a friend and poet who had died; in order to do it
he became a Greek shepherd, mourning another one." Surveying
the stanzaic form and rhyme scheme of the poem, however,
Ransom finds certain irregularities that violate the classical model,
and he decides that these must have been *intended* by Milton, not
because they make points within the form of the poem but because
it was Milton's way of asserting his own superiority to the established forms. "They are defiances, showing the man unwilling
to give way to the poet; they are not based upon a special issue but
upon surliness, and general principles." This assertion of personality, he declares, makes Milton a modern poet, who rebels
against the traditional forms. He suggests that Milton first wrote
the poem in regular stanzas, then went back and deliberately
roughened it.

Forms and ceremonies, Ransom says, constitute the pure
artistry; but the modern poet, fearful of monotony, would violate
them enough to call attention to himself as artist. Milton is master
of many forms within the poem, and uses them all with great vir-
tuosity; but at times he refuses to remain within them, and asserts
himself directly, as in his censure of the English clergy. Though it is

done in the speech of Saint Peter, he "drops his Latinity for plain speech, where he can express a Milton who is angry, violent, and perhaps a little bit vulgar. It is the first time in his career that we have seen in him a taste for writing at this level." In the years immediately following Milton would write other poems displaying such anger, and prose as well, before returning for good to the formal anonymity of the great epics.

Ransom makes one more conjecture. He notes that after the speaker of the poem expresses his bitter thoughts on the futility of art—"Alas! what boots it with incessant care / To tend the homely slighted shepherd's trade, / And strictly meditate the thankless Muse?"—and asks whether it were not a better idea to do as others do and pleasure oneself, Milton violates the monologue convention of the poem for the only time. Having said that "Fame is the spur" and pointed out that instead of fame there comes Death, "the blind Fury with the abhorr'd shears," to nullify it, he interrupts the monologue with a speech by Phoebus. "'But not the praise,' / Phoebus replied, and touched my trembling ears." Phoebus goes on to speak of Fame as residing in immortality. Milton then resumes the monologue and concludes his poem.

In violating the elegiac form here, Ransom says, Milton again asserts his individuality, and not without accident is it in a passage on fame: "In his disrespect of [the form] he can be the person, the John Milton who is different, and dangerous, and very likely to become famous." In this instance Milton is again the modern poet who "does not propose to be buried beneath his own elegy." The danger is that in so asserting his personality the poet will overreach himself. He violates the artistic illusion, and if he is not careful, we become aware that he has "counterfeited the excitement" and we are "pained and let down."

"Lycidas, for the most part a work of great art," Ransom concludes, "is sometimes artful and tricky"; and we are made "disturbingly conscious of a man behind the artist."

In "Forms and Citizens" Ransom begins by leaving Milton in order to discuss forms and rituals, in both poetry and society. Poetry is one of the aesthetic forms that a society hands down. Unlike economic forms these "do not serve the principle of utility." They are "play-forms," not "work-forms." The economic forms, by contrast, are of intense practicality, and are "the recipes of maximum efficiency, short routes to 'success,' to welfare, to the attainment of natural satisfactions and comforts." In earlier societies play-forms were as important as work-forms. The aesthetic forms

were "techniques of restraint," standing "between the individual
and his natural object" and imposing "a check upon his action."
Modern society [here read Industrialism], with its horror of
"empty" forms and ceremonies, may well be exposing its social
solidarity "to the anarchy of too much greed."

Art, like manners, Ransom continues, imposes an aesthetic
distance between individual and object; it proposes a form.
Without the form we have desire directly acted upon, as in the
savage who covets the woman. But manners require that the social
man approach the woman "with ceremony, and pay her a fas-
tidious courtship." The woman, contemplated under restraint, becomes "a person and an aesthetic object; therefore a richer object." The function of a code of manners, therefore, is to civilize
and to enrich, thus making us "capable of something better than
the stupidity of an appetitive or economic life."

In the same way, Ransom says, a religious ceremony, by forcing
the bereaved to contemplate his loss through ritual and form, both
expands and lightens the grief, mitigating its explosive or
obsessional quality, and giving him the "grateful sense that his
community supports him in a dreadful hour." The pageantry dis-
pels his preoccupation with the deadness of the body.

Society through its forms, rituals, ceremonies, and conventions
chooses "to graft upon the economic relation a vast increment of
diffuse and irrelevant sensibilia, and keep it there forever, obstruct-
ing science and action." It stands between the animal and his
desire; it makes possible contemplation, aesthetic pleasure. It is,
therefore, our civilization. The function of art is thus to "frustrate
the natural man and induce the aesthetic one." Art "wants us to
enjoy life, to taste and reflect as we drink," rather than to gulp it
down; and so its technique must be artificial, as the techniques of
manners or rituals are. The poet, having to take account of his
form, is delayed and hindered in describing the object, and is thus
able to apprehend its existence in its own sake and not merely as an
object to be unthinkingly possessed. Art rests on formalism, as do
religion and manners, so that "a natural affiliation binds together
the gentleman, the religious man, and the artist—punctilious
characters, all of them, in their formalism." Ransom takes up
Eliot's famous pronouncement—"in politics, royalism; in religion,
Anglo-Catholic; in literature, classical"—and suggests his own version: "in manners, aristocratic; in religion, ritualistic; in art, traditional." He urges his generation to emphasize the "formal" emphasis as a way of cultivating the natural man: "The object of a

proper society," he says, "is to instruct its members how to transform instinctive experience into aesthetic experience."

Ransom goes on to say that religion exists for its ritual, not its doctrine, for the doctrinal issues are "really insoluble for human logic." "The only solution that is possible, since the economic solution is not possible, is the aesthetic one." He describes some of the occasions of human experience in which the aesthetic experience is appropriate—occasions in which contemplation rather than economic possession is desirable. Then he distinguishes between two kinds of contemplation, the scientific and the artistic. The scientist would study the object in order to control it; he is like the caveman and the economic man in the sense that his ultimate objective is possession. The artist, by contrast, would contemplate the object neither for immediate nor future possession, but only to know it for its own properties. His knowledge of the object is therefore a kind of "knowledge so radical that the scientist as a scientist can scarcely understand it, and puzzles to see it rendered, richly and wastefully, in the poem, or the painting."

At this point we might pause to note several things. One is that Ransom has contrasted religious and aesthetic knowledge with scientific and economic knowledge, in that they are not aimed at useful possession but at formal contemplation. He has furthermore equated civilization with such contemplation. The raw economic desire to possess, or the more sophisticated scientific knowledge which is nonetheless aimed at just such efficient economic possession, are at the service of the natural animal, but only the civilized man can enjoy the formal, ritualistic, aesthetic or religious knowledge, which is not predatory. What is especially interesting, if we think of the possible relationship of this discussion to his Agrarian interests, is that he chooses to use the word *economic* to designate practicality, "short routes to 'success,' " "to the attainment of natural satisfactions and comforts." The implication is that insofar as a society must concern itself with economics it is to that extent therefore *not* aesthetic, *not* artistic—not civilized. Therefore, to the degree that economics must be considered in an Agrarian (or any other) program, the program is to that degree *un*aesthetic, even opposed to the aesthetic forms. And it also appears self-evident that someone who happens to be chiefly concerned with aesthetic forms will not be rendering his own true account by continuing to concern himself with the economic forms. In short, Ransom has put culture and economics at opposite poles, and there can be little doubt where his own sympathies lie.

Let me continue now with Ransom on Milton, which I intend to
suggest is also Ransom *as* Milton, or Ransom on Ransom. The man
Milton, Ransom says, "is a strong man, and has intense economic
persuasions, if we may bring under that term his personal, moral,
and political principles." Though his poetry deals with these principles, it does not do so *as* poetry; for as poetry the situations dealt
with are "fancied ones which do not touch him so nearly." Milton
may be found to have confronted his economic persuasions "more
precisely or practically somewhere in his economic prose; that is, in
the ethical, theological, political tracts." In "Lycidas" he was the
poet, though sometimes he found it difficult to repress the economic man, and these are the less artistically successful elements of
the poem. But though he felt the economic considerations of his
time strongly, and was naturally inclined to deal with them and
sometimes did so very strongly indeed, "he knew of this tendency
in himself and opposed it." He did not choose finally to define
himself as a man, but as an artist. "As a man he was too much like
any of us; if not too appetitive in the flesh, at least too zealous in intellectual action, which comes aesthetically to the same thing."
But as an artist he was John Milton.

Milton did, as man, have one blind spot. Like many a modern
man he was suspicious and truculent toward ritual. Had he been a
Catholic rather than a Protestant, Ransom suggests, or perhaps an
Anglo-Catholic, he would not have felt such suspicion and trucu-
lence. "So inveterate and passionate did this resistance become
that it took him into the extremist Protestant camp to write hard
doctrine, and actually to set up his own religion as a project in dialectic," even though "all the time he 'knew' better." (Here we
might keep in mind that the author of that observation was also the
author of *God without Thunder: An Unorthodox Defense of Orthodoxy*.) But as it turned out, this did not matter, for as a poet he
used ritual and understood it well, even though in its public,
political form he resisted it. Milton made his choice and became
the artist.

We do not regret his decision when we have to follow him during the ten
or fifteen years after 1640, the period when he felt obliged as a citizen to
drop the poet and become the preacher, the tractarian, and the economic
man. During that period we remember gratefully that he shares our own
view of his intractable nature, in which so much of the sin of Adam
resides; that he understands his predicament. The formality of poetry sus-
tained him, induced in him his highest nobility, and his most delicate feeling. The ding-dong of contemporary controversy brought out of him

something ugly and plebian that was there all the time, waiting. He took
care that the preacher should be the Miltonic rôle for but a period; the
artist came back, and may have been the better artist for the ignominy
which he had suffered; though I shall not try to argue that.

Ransom concludes with a justification of the rightness of Milton's
decision to be the artist, saying that art "is a career, precisely as
science is a career. It is as serious, it has an attitude as official, it is as
studied and consecutive, it is by all means as difficult, it is no less
important." The Milton who matters is the poet. "Milton is the
poetry."

What I propose is that, in these two essays on John Milton's
poetry, Ransom was very actively pondering his own situation.
Whether or not "Lycidas" is "a poem nearly anonymous," it seems
clear that in their authorship these essays are only partly anonymous, and that John Ransom the man is, I think quite inten-
tionally, declining to give entire precedence to John Ransom the
explicator of poems. For Milton is not the only poet in the English
language who had as poet taken a pastoral role to deliver himself
from "the scrivener's son, the Master of Arts [from Oxford, not
Cambridge, to be sure], the handsome and finicky young man."
Not merely Milton has been suspected of going over a smoothly
written poem and deliberately coarsening it. Not merely Milton,
having concluded the poems of his apprenticeship, had found
himself "uneasy, skeptical, about the whole foundation of poetry
as an art." Not merely Milton discovered that the "point of view of
. . . shepherds, as romantic innocents and rustics, is excellent, and
offers a wide range of poetic discourse concerning friendship, love,
nature, and even, a startling innovation . . . the 'ruin of the
clergy' " (cf. "Armageddon"). John Ransom too tried sonnets, also
ballads ("Piazza Piece" and "Captain Carpenter.")

Milton was not the only artist that Ransom knew who was "capable of perfect logic." Ransom too was a strongly passionate
man, with "intense personal, moral and political principles," who
treated the major concerns of his poetry at other times in "his economic prose; that is, in the ethical, theological, political tracts."
Like Milton, Ransom was "a man of his times and held strong
views upon the contemporary ecclesiastical and political situation,
in a period when the church and the political order was undergoing
revolution." He too had "a natural inclination to preach, and display his zeal; to preach upon such themes as the reform of the
clergy, and the reform of the government," and "knew of this
tendency in himself and opposed it." It can probably be assumed

that this son and grandson of Methodist ministers "went so far as to abandon that career in the church which his father had intended for him and to which he seems at first to have consented." Ransom the dialectician was "if not too appetitive in the flesh, at least too zealous in intellectual action, which comes aesthetically to the same thing." And so on, even down to Ransom having for a period of some years "felt obliged as a citizen to drop the poet and become the preacher, the tractarian, and the economic man." I am not at all convinced that Ransom's depiction of Milton corresponds to the biographical John Milton; but beyond a doubt it corresponds to the situation of John Crowe Ransom in the early 1930s.

He had gotten involved in Agrarianism because by the late 1920s he had come to the stage at which he could no longer separate the writing of poems from theorizing about the nature of poetry and of art, and his aesthetic thinking had led straight into more thinking about religion and the good society. Long before Ransom became an Agrarian in any conscious sense he had written certain poems, notably "Armageddon," "Conrad at Twilight," and "Antique Harvesters," in which the ideas and attitudes in *God without Thunder* and his Agrarian writings had been largely worked out as images. After Ransom reached those conclusions, he had ceased to write much new verse. In the early and middle 1920s he had produced new poem after new poem, but after "Antique Harvesters" (1925) he wrote comparatively few poems.

It is interesting that this poem, in which he unites for the first time the themes of the South, religion, ritual, and agriculture in a single poem, is quite unlike most of Ransom's poetry in that it lacks the customary ironic qualification of the speaker's position. The speaker takes a stand from the outset, and he does not proceed to develop ironic counterpoint between meaning and language. As Vivienne Koch remarks, the poem "shows Ransom triumphing on purely poetic grounds over his own critical notions concerning poetry and belief."[5] She proclaims it "a conquest of structure by texture"—meaning that the language requires the reader to accept the idea, rather than scoring points off it as Ransom almost always does in his poems (and as he says is essential to the nature of poetry). In its assertion of belief, and its unqualified identification of the speaker with the assertion, it is as "patriotic" a poem as any that Donald Davidson ever wrote.

[5]"The Achievement of John Crowe Ransom," *Sewanee Review*, 58 (1950), 255.

I do not think this is an accident. I believe that the writing of "Antique Harvesters" signifies Ransom's arrival at a point in his career at which he has decided where he stands in the cosmos. He has made his allegiances, and elaborated the ceremonies. The long exploration for the meaning of his experience that he began in his poetry back with the early lyrics of *Poems about God* is almost concluded. Given Ransom's particular kind of sensibility, he could not dissociate what he did while writing a poem from what he did as thinker and logician. The logic, the poetry, the religious and social belief had to operate together. Having reached the position in his poetry, he now had to work it out logically, in prose, and this he did. Another kind of poet—Davidson, for example—might go right on writing poem after poem designed to promulgate his belief. But not Ransom: except for "Antique Harvesters" he was not that sort of poet.

So, with several brilliant exceptions, such as "Painted Head" and "Prelude to an Evening," Ransom had all but finished his work as a poet when he had reached the position in his thinking denoted by "Antique Harvesters." He plunged into Agrarianism, and for the next half-dozen years and more he was "the preacher, the tractarian, and the economic man."

Yet if Ransom had come to Agrarianism as the *locus* of art, the image of the country where the ceremony of poetry is possible, as in a predatory industrial society it was not possible, it would follow that there should not be any conflict between Agrarianism and poetry, but rather the opposite. What he found, however, was that in responding to the attacks on *I'll Take My Stand* as an impractical affair, he had to immerse himself in economics. It turned out, therefore, that one could not have the vision of the Agrarian society as the place for poetry and ritual, if the economics was unrealistic. So the economics came under logical scrutiny. And when Ransom, with that very logical and dialectical mind of his, began examining the economics, what he began finding, however reluctantly, was that the Agrarianism didn't really make much sense as a literal economic prescription for the South.

Well before the time of the publication of the second symposium, *Who Owns America?*, in 1936, Ransom is changing his position. In his contribution to that symposium, "What Does the South Want?," we find him asserting that "there are business men and laborers, equally with farmers, to be defended," and there is "practically nobody, even in the economically backward South, who proposes to destroy corporate business. Least of all, it may be, in the South, which wants to see its industries developed, so that it may be permitted to approach closer to regional autonomy."[6] It turns out that what is wrong is not corporate business, not industry, but Big Business, predatory industry.

It also turns out that farming is, after all, appropriately viewed as a business, not an aesthetic ceremony; and its difficulty is that it "is an overcapitalized business, therefore an overproductive business, and therefore an unprofitable one." Unlike the industrialist the farmer cannot destroy his excess of fixed capital, since his capital is the land. Therefore the farmer should strive for self-sufficiency, and for the federal government to come to his aid by lowering and even eliminating his taxes, and provide a great deal more services for him than it now does, such as rural free electrification. As for the laboring man, he should have his job made secure, and unemployment insurance if he is out of work. The standard of living should be raised in industrial communities, with indoor plumbing, pavements, playgrounds, parks, adequate medical and hospital services, and so on.

By the year 1936, in other words, John Ransom has become no economic conservative at all, but a good New Dealer, and such, I believe, he would remain for the remainder of his long life. Davidson was quite right when he wrote to Tate in late March of 1937 that Ransom "seemed to me (when I talked with him) definitely to be giving the signal for a crossroads at which he takes a turn to the left." What has happened is that Ransom's essential economic and political realism has won out over his poetic view of the Agrarian South. The Agrarianism, and the South, therefore no longer fit into his image of the only proper country for poetry, the place for ritual and ceremony and belief. For if the South is industrializing, and *should* industrialize because economically it must, then it isn't the South that can provide the place for the aesthetic ceremony any better than some other place could—preferably some small place, politically-enlightened, but with the fine arts and the humanities very much honored there. A place, let us say, such as a small liberal arts college, not located in a big city but in the country, and where there is a definite commitment to ritual and ceremony—a small Episcopal college it might even be.

Of course I do not suggest that it happened nearly so logically and consciously as that. This would leave out fortuitous circum-

---

[6] *Who Owns America?: A Declaration of Independence*, ed. Herbert Agar and Allen Tate (Boston: Houghton Mifflin, 1936), p. 185.

stances, and finances, and numerous other considerations. The truth is that Ransom was tired of southern Agrarianism, weary of writing economic articles; and he wanted to get back to poetry—if not to writing it, then in any event to writing and thinking about it. So long as he stayed in Nashville and at Vanderbilt, the old allegiances and associates would be very much present, and to turn away from being "the preacher, the tractarian, and the economic man" would be all the harder. Therefore the prospect of a clean break, at a small college "of the Ohio the bank dexter" rather than the "bank sinister," where he could be professor of poetry and only that, came to seem very attractive indeed. Whereupon he joined the faculty of Kenyon College.

Being John Ransom, however, even that was not enough. It was necessary for him to bring his logic into order, to work out the matter in accord with the fullest extension of the logical implication. Ransom was no one to leave inconsistencies unresolved, to permit areas of thought within the logical framework to remain unexamined. So it was not sufficient that he give up his Agrarian allegiance; he also had to repudiate it. What is interesting are the terms on which he went about doing so. In the *Kenyon Review* for fall 1945 he published "Art and the Human Economy," commenting on two other essays in that issue on religion and poetry. He remarks of one of them that the author, W. P. Southard, "taxes the Southern agrarians for not having practiced what they preached," by being unwilling to live an agrarian life as well as write about it. Ransom remarks that "without consenting to [a] division of labor, and hence modern society, we should have not only no effective science, invention, and scholarship, but nothing to speak of in art, e.g., *reviews* and contributions to *reviews*, fine poems and their exegesis" (italics Ransom's). Branches of knowledge, products of civilization, constitute science, "and are the guilty fruits" of our society. "The arts are the expiations, but they are beautiful. . . . They seem worth the vile welter through which homeless spirits must wade between times, with sensibilities subject to ravage as they are." Such are the only practical terms on which the human economy can now operate.

The Agrarians, he admitted, "did not go back to the farm. . . . And presently it seemed to them that they could not invite other moderns, their business friends for example, to do what they were not doing themselves." He found it ironical that the recently announced Declaration of Potsdam proposed that when the war was won Germany should be stripped of its industry and the German people forced to take up an agrarian economy. "Once I should have thought there could have been no greater happiness for a people, but now I have no difficulty in seeing it for what it was meant to be: a heavy punishment."

Ransom went on to declare that the "agrarian nostalgia" had been valuable to the participants. And he found it interesting that now, whatever the politics of the individual Agrarians might be, "it may be observed that they are defending the freedom of the arts, whose function they understand. Not so much can be said for some intemperate exponents of the economic 'progress.' "[7]

As might have been expected, Donald Davidson was outraged, the more so, as he wrote to Tate on October 3, 1945, that Ransom had sent him a copy of the *Kenyon Review*, "the only copy I have ever received from John since he began editing it, except for one copy I earned for my one and only review contributed." Clearly Ransom had wished to notify his former colleague and fellow Agrarian of his recantation. What most annoyed Davidson was that "John accepts as a valid interpretation of our principles the silliest and meanest version of our ideas that our critics gave. . . . He even accepts the 'nostalgia' part as authentic. . . . I can only say, what devil has got into John Ransom?"

Ransom's version of what Agrarianism had involved did indeed make the assumption that the Agrarians had wanted the South to remain agricultural in order that they might enjoy the fruits of such a society as a place for writing poetry. And of course there was a great deal more to Agrarianism than that; the whole thrust of the movement as a protest against dehumanization is left out of such a diagnosis. But from the standpoint of Ransom's own involvement in *I'll Take My Stand* and the ensuing enterprise, there was, to make a bad pun, more truth than poetry to what he said. He *had* gotten involved in Agrarianism by the route of aesthetic theory and his southern allegiance; and his agrarian activity had been a way of asserting, in social and economic terms, the need for the society of ceremony and belief. When he had been forced to examine his economic assumptions, to face up to what for him was the actuality of an agrarian society, he had found that—*in the terms that he had conceived of it*—Agrarianism had been only a romantic dream after all, a land of the heart's desire where the ceremony of poetry could be possible, and which was not the twentieth-century South

[7] *Beating the Bushes: Selected Essays 1941–1970* (New York: New Directions, 1972), pp. 133–34.

he lived and worked in at all. The fusion of ritual and region, art and religion that he had set forth in "Antique Harvesters" was only, after all, the image for a poem. The poetry was not the South; in that case he would go with the poetry. Thus the *Kenyon Review*—and the New Criticism. He even went so far as to propose to omit "Antique Harvesters" from his next collection of poems; Tate, to whom he sent the manuscript, had to insist that so fine a poem not be victimized for the sake of "logical consistency."

There was still one more exploration necessary, however, and Ransom soon made it. If Agrarianism was not a reality, and a poet had to live and work in twentieth-century industrial society, what did that make of the poet's place in society? As the keeper of ritual, the creator of ceremonies, of course, using the forms to infuse into the consciousness the kind of knowledge that only the arts could provide, which is to say knowledge without desire, knowledge of the world's body, the object for and of itself. He wrote a number of essays to enforce this position, of which "Poetry: A Note on Ontology" was the first and perhaps the best. But a poet had to live somewhere. So he developed another theory, which he elucidated in "The Communities of Letters" (1952). The kind of knowledge of the world that the poet offers, knowledge without desire, can *only* be apprehended aesthetically; it cannot be translated literally into the public world. But if the vision of the poet is wise and true, he acquires readers who will share with each other the enjoyment of the knowledge of the world he offers and who will thus constitute a community of letters. "How much more tolerant, and more humane, is this community than the formal society!" The public of each and any important writer constitutes such a community: "it is one of those minority cultural groups which have their rights in a free society as surely as individuals do." And though this community of letters has no corporate boundaries and no economics, it is real, and together with the other communities of letters makes up a kind of "secondary society branching off from the formal or primary society."[8] To use another metaphor which Ransom has used, we thus have "pockets of culture," with the hope that they may become more numerous and more widespread. This is a long way from the vision of the southern agrarian community, with its farmers becoming philosophers. But it is nevertheless a community, and so we might say that Ransom still managed to find a community role for his poets.

[8] *Poems and Essays* (New York: Vintage Books, 1955), p. 116.

If, in writing about John Milton returning to his muse after a tractarian and economic period, Ransom did envision himself being able to do the same, then his expectation was not borne out. After leaving Vanderbilt he published no more poetry save for his Harvard Phi Beta Kappa poem, "Address to the Scholars of New England" (1939). In the 1960s, following his retirement as editor of the *Kenyon Review,* he began revising a few of his earlier poems, with results that can only be termed appalling. Happily his publisher declined to excise the earlier versions from the several editions of his *Selected Poems;* both the older versions and the revisions were included. Why it was that Ransom decided to do this, I have no idea. But doubtless he did; however illogical anything John Ransom did, he always had a logical reason for it. Allen Tate is accurate in describing "his compulsive revisions as a quite consistent activity—as an extension of his reliance on *logic* as the ultimate standard of judgment."[9]

Similarly any explanation of why it was that Ransom did not write much new poetry after the 1920s must remain in the realm of conjecture. My own theory is that when Ransom insisted critically that poetry was *knowledge,* he was describing its function for himself; when he wrote a poem, it was an organic, functioning part of a reasoning process that was going on in his mind, and what happened by the late twenties was that he had more or less figured out for himself what he wanted to know. When he described poetry as civilizing desire by forcing formal expression upon it and thus changing it from animal appetite into knowledge without desire, he was saying something about his own complex nature as man and poet. I think that the ceremony of poetry had the result of making Ransom see the world and his place in it differently, making possible a kind of disciplined mastery over himself and his mind, so that he could *thenceforth* be content with the rational method of logic as his way of ordering his experience. There was subsequently no role, *for Ransom,* for the poetry to perform. Through writing poetry he wrote himself out of the need to write it.

In this context I would note a remark of Ransom's in "The Tense of Poetry," which was first published in the *Southern Review* in 1935. Ransom is postulating a history of the human race in respect to language. First is the Golden Age when prose and poetry were one. Then came the historical epochs when the two kinds of dis-

[9]"Reflections on the Death of John Crowe Ransom," *Sewanee Review,* 82 (1974), 549–50.

course diverged, with prose becoming the language of business, morality, and science, and poetry set itself up to stand against these. The third, the modern age comes when prose has taken over all the objects that it thinks worth claiming, and poetry must become difficult and strange, torturing itself in order to be poetry at all. The prose, he concludes, "is located . . . in our own minds, *which have acquired such a prose habit that those parts which are not active in prose are thoroughly suppressed,* and can hardly break through and exercise themselves" (italics mine).[10] The key word, I think, is *suppressed.* It is almost as if the poetry has been kept throttled and under control in order that the prose could keep on doing its job.

If so we can only say that however much the suppression may have deprived us of more poetry, it was in a very good cause and we are more than willing to accept the deprivation, in return for the distinguished critical writing and editing that this man performed during the several decades after his fiftieth year. If he forsook the muse, or vice versa, he did not, as writer of criticism, abandon the ceremonious language. "John Ransom," in Allen Tate's words, "wrote the most perspicious, the most engaging, and the most elegant prose of all the poet-critics of our time."[11]

He died on July 3, 1974, at the age of eighty-six. One might quote from his own poem, "Captain Carpenter," for an epitaph:

> I thought him Sirs an honest gentleman
> Citizen husband soldier and scholar enow
> Let jangling kites eat of him if they can.

[10] *The World's Body,* p. 237.
[11] "Reflections on the Death of John Crowe Ransom," p. 551.

The Evolution of Ransom's Critical Theory Image and Idea

Thomas Daniel Young

IN THE FALL of 1937 John Crowe Ransom published "Criticism, Inc.," his best-known critical essay, in which he sets forth what he calls the "proper business of criticism." For too long, he protests, our critics have been amateurs, men without the specific qualifications to perform the highly specialized functions that they have undertaken. The kinds of competence a critic needs could be expected to come from one of three sources, but none of these has produced the sort of precise and systematic criticism needed to permit literature to convey the unique kind of knowledge it possesses. The first group of "trained performers" from which a reader might reasonably expect the kind of assistance that he requires is the artist himself, but results from this source have often been disappointing. The artist is not necessarily a reliable critic, for even though he "should know good art when he sees it," his "understanding is often intuitive rather than dialectical." As long as he sticks to the technical effects of the art works with which he is familiar, his commentary is usually valuable; but often when he attempts to expound a theory of art his critical weaknesses are glaringly apparent. The second source from which sound criticism should derive is the philosopher. But the philosopher, who should know "all about the function of the fine arts," is not always a dependable critic. He is weak where the artist is strong: he can expound a theory of art, but he is usually not well enough acquainted with individual works to comment on specific technical effects.

Since the reader of poetry can get the kind of critical assistance that he needs from neither the artist nor the philosopher, to whom should he turn? The logical source of the kind of help he needs and deserves is the university professor of English. But those readers who look to the universities for this kind of help, Ransom warns, will surely be disappointed. The professors of English are "learned but not critical men"; it would seem that they have "appropriated every avenue of escape from their responsibility" that is either decent or official. They spend a lifetime compiling the "data of literature" and rarely if ever commit themselves to a literary judgment. Some of them are good textual, philological, and historical scholars, but few can or will provide the precise and systematic criticism the work of art demands. Ransom calls, therefore, for a Criticism, Incorporated, in order that this important activity may be "taken in hand by professionals."

This essay has often been cited as the clarion call for the New Criticism, an appeal for a new approach to literary study, for criticism concerned with formal analysis and literary judgments, with the insights which come only from an intensive study of the poem itself. Obviously Ransom is defining the kind of criticism which he thought absolutely essential if literature is to retain a significant role in the life of civilized man. But it was not a new criticism. He merely defined formally the approach to literature that he himself had been advocating and practicing for more than twenty years when this essay appeared.

In February 1914 he had outlined in a letter to his father a theory of poetics, which he had worked out in many conversations with Samuel C. Chew, who at that time was his colleague on the faculty of the Hotchkiss School in Lakeville, Connecticut. In the teaching of Latin poetry, Ransom wrote his father, he was able to recognize a good translation of Virgil, because the translation is poetry, even if it does not contain meter. Although everyone would admit that poetry in its most nearly complete form employs meter, what else it contains has not been formulated, and the best place to study this question is in a good translation of the poetry of another language. If one sets out to determine how a translation that "satisfies good taste" differs from "correct and formal" prose, he will make several interesting discoveries. He will find, first of all, that the "good translation preserves the discontinuities, ellipses, the failing to attain preciseness and perfect connection" because the "mode of thought that is imaginative rather than logical or scientific" is induced through the use of words "which mean the given thing yet involve it in accidental associations that provoke the imagination." Even the meter is calculated to induce the imaginative rather than the logical mode because words "have a double nature: they stand for things and are associated inseparably with thought." Although in prose the author may be unconscious of the sound of his words, in poetry he provides a musical arrangement of words within which is fitted as much of the intended meaning as possible. The musical requirement, however, is usually so restrictive that the choice of words to convey the meaning is severely limited; therefore the poet must deploy words "which fail of precision and introduce extraneous color and distract the attention and suggest beautiful enterprises of the imagination." As soon as he could develop his poetic theory in detail, Ransom concluded, he hoped to demonstrate that there is an "inevitable union between poetic form and what is called poetic imagination."

During the fall and winter of 1913–1914, almost ten years before his first essay in literary theory appeared, Ransom's basic concept of the nature and function of the poetic structure was already fixed in his mind. This rudimentary discussion of the dual role of words in the poetic translation anticipates by more than twenty years his definition of the poem, in "Wanted: An Ontological Critic (1941), as a "loose logical structure with a good deal of local texture." The poem may be differentiated from the prose discourse on the basis of this "odd structure." Over the years he would attempt to designate exactly how the poem "differs from the prose discourse." It is, he insisted more than once, an *order* rather than a *kind* of content that "distinguishes texture from structure and poetry from prose." The differentia of poetry as discourse is an ontological one; its nature differs from that of the prose discourse because it serves a different purpose. The suggestion presented in this early letter—that poetry attempts to "induce the mode of thought that is imaginative rather than logical"—is an obvious, if an incomplete and inexact statement of his defense of poetry as a means of cognition, not of instruction. "Poetry intends," he wrote in 1941, near the middle of his career, "to recover the denser and more refractory original world which we know loosely through our perceptions and memories." It is "ontologically distinct" because it is the "kind of knowledge by which we must know what we have arranged that we shall not know otherwise."[1]

These two concepts, the foundation upon which almost all of his later aesthetic speculation was based, were extracted, Ransom later admitted, from Aristotle, Plato, Plautus, Kant, Hegel, Schopenhauer, and Coleridge, some of the thinkers whom he had studied regularly since his undergraduate days at Vanderbilt and particularly at Oxford, where he had read the Greats. These ideas were first formulated and given tentative expression in conversations with the members of the Hermit Crabs, a literary club he had organized at Oxford in 1911. In the discussions with Samuel Chew,

[1] *The World's Body* (New York: Scribners, 1938), p. x.

who had diverted his attention from the classics to English literature, they began to assume the basic form in which they would be
published many years later. His first real interest in literary theorizing, which began in 1913, the year he taught at the Hotchkiss
School, was stimulated so much by his associations with Allen
Tate, Donald Davidson, and the other Fugitives at Vanderbilt that
by the mid-1920s criticism was claiming the major part of his creative energies. During the last year of its existence the *Fugitive,*
which was published in Nashville from 1922 to 1925, provided him
the opportunity to express for publication some of the critical ideas
which had been slowly evolving over the past ten or more years. In
the first of these essays Ransom presents in essence the views that
would comprise the introduction to *The World's Body,* published
nearly fifteen years later. "The respectable attainments of much
recent poetry," he wrote in "Mixed Modes" (March 1925), "exist
to controvert the view that poets are essentially juveniles." Such a
view, he insisted, might have been entertained in 1900, at the close
of a century of the simplest poetry in English literary history, but
this is not *the* literary tradition. For the real literary tradition one
must go back beyond the "nonsense melodies of Swinburne," the
"sinister naiveté of the pre-Raphaelites," even further back than
Tennyson, Browning, and the English romantic poets to the time
when a poet could "devote a complete act of cerebration to each
of his poetical themes," to the age of Chaucer, Spenser, Shakespeare, and Milton when the poet could "put his whole mind and
experience to work in poetry." If poetry is to be the kind of activity
that will engage the mind of an adult, he concludes, it cannot be
the "paregoric of lullaby." The poets "must report their own
mixed modes," not attempt "to simplify and prettify the theme."[2]
They must produce a kind of poetry, as Ransom said in *The
World's Body* (1938), that "will appeal to persons who have aged
in the "pure intellectual disciplines" and cannot "play innocent
without feeling very foolish."[3]

Two other essays published in the *Fugitive* later the same year
demonstrate quite clearly that by the mid-1920s Ransom was very
near to establishing critical positions he would never abandon. In
"Thoughts on the Poetic Discontent" (June 1925) he sets up the
conflict between science and art by suggesting some of the
differences between the knowledge acquired by the scientific

[2]"Mixed Modes," *Fugitive,* 4 (1925), 29.
[3]*The World's Body,* p. viii.

method and the knowledge resulting from an analytical study of poetry and the other arts. This brief note not only contains a clear statement of this basic distinction, one essential in the evolution of his mature theories, but it includes as well the germ of some of his most sophisticated critical concepts. In his intellectual development, Ransom suggests early in this essay, man moves through three stages. Beginning as a dualist, aware both of the "world without and the spirit within," he proceeds through a period of monism (in which he attempts to set up a mystical union with God and nature) before he reaches a third stage, one in which a reaffirmation of dualism occurs. But now he is a "dualist with a difference"; he possesses a "mellow wisdom which we may call irony." This state "presupposes the others" because it implies a "strenuous period of romantic creation" and then a rejection of all romantic forms. But this rejection is neither easy nor complete; it is arrived at so unwillingly that there "lingers . . . much of the music and color and romantic mystery which is perhaps the absolute poetry." In the second essay, "Prose: A Doctrine of Relativity" (September 1925), he argues that a poem has many meanings. In addition to its fable, which often is not as innocent as it looks, there may be dozens of words and phrases to lead the mind away from the poem's logical content and into seemingly irrelevant excursions. But here the differences between poetry and scientific discourse become apparent. Poetry uses the "widest terms" possible, science the narrowest; and these terms "function precisely to evoke in our memories the deepest previous experience." Thus poetry is art, not science; and its reference is "always free and personal," never "fixed and ideal."[4]

During the late 1920s, then, Ransom was working toward the complete articulation of the aesthetic principles upon which he would establish his ontological theory of criticism. During these years he was engaged in an important correspondence with Allen Tate which allowed him to test and refine his artistic speculations under the penetrating scrutiny of one of the most active critical minds of the twentieth century. In a letter written in December 1923, as a part of his explanation of why he found the poetry of T. S. Eliot difficult, Ransom again attempted to describe the unique nature of the art object:

The art-thing sounds like the first immediate transcript of reality, but it isn't; it's a long way from the event. It isn't the raw stuff of experience.

[4]"Prose: A Doctrine of Relativity," *Fugitive*, 4 (1925), 93.

The passion in it has mellowed down—emotion recollected in *tranquility*, etc. Above all things else, the core of experience in the record has been taken up into the sum total of things and its relations there discovered are given in the works of art. That is why the marginal meanings, the associations, the interlinear element of a poem are all-important. The most delicate piece of work that a poet has to do is to avoid a misleading connection in his phrasing. There must not be a trace of the expository philosophical method, but nevertheless the substance of the philosophical conclusion must be there for the intelligent reader.

In addition to an apparent effort to express what he will later call the structure-texture formulation of the poem, one can detect in this statement an interest in identifying the unique characteristics of the poetic structure through an examination of the creative process itself.

By the late 1920s Ransom was convinced that the ideas which had been slowly surfacing for almost a decade had developed sufficiently to require an extensive essay to give them adequate expression; consequently he spent the better part of a year on an essay which he called "The Third Moment." After months of almost uninterrupted writing he completed a manuscript of two hundred pages, which during the next several years he revised many times, trying to get it in shape for publication. Finally he decided that it was hopelessly abstract, that such a study could be "pursued only in the constant company of the actual poems"; therefore, as he said ten years later, he "had the pleasure of consigning it to the flames." Since no copy of this manuscript exists, its contents must be reconstructed from the letters that Ransom wrote Allen Tate during the period of its composition. On September 5, 1926, he discussed in some detail what he was trying to do. There are, this letter begins, "three moments in the historical order of experience": the first is the actual experience itself, "pure of all intellectual content, unreflective, concrete, and singular; there are no distinctions and the subject is identical with the whole." In the second moment "cognition takes place," and a record must be made of the first moment. This record is made by way of "*concepts* discovered in cognition." This is the beginning of science with its intent upon practicality and its compulsion to produce abstractions through subtracting parts from the whole experience. Only in the third moment are we "aware of the deficiency of the record"; only then do we realize that "most of [the] experience is quite missing from it." All "our concepts" and "all our histories" combined can never restore the whole experience.

That "fugitive first moment" can be recovered only through images; it cannot be reproduced through philosophical synthesis:

How can we get back to that first moment? There is only one answer: by images. The Imagination is the faculty of Pure Memory, or unconscious mind; it brings out the original experiences from the dark storeroom, where we dwell upon them with a joy proportionate to our previous despair. And therefore, when we make images, we are regressive; we are trying to reconstitute an experience which we once had, only to handle and mutilate. Only, we cannot quite reconstitute them. Association is too strong for us; the habit of cognition is too strong. The images come out mixed and adulterated with concepts. . . . We are not really opposed to science, except as it monopolizes and warps us; we are perfectly content to dwell in the phenomenal world for much of our time; this is to be specifically human; we would not be babes nor beasts; we require merely the fulness of life, which is existence in the midst of all our faculties.

Man tries, then, to reconstitute the elusive first moment in all its concrete particularity through fancies (or daydreams), dreams, religion, morals, and art. Ransom concludes this lengthy explication of his theory by offering again his definition of poetry, this time calling it the "exhibit of Opposition and at the same time Reconciliation between the Conceptual or Formal and the Individual or Concrete." This is his earliest statement of his concept of the Concrete Universal, which is developed in two essays in the mid-1950s and in his last published essay, written in 1970.

The "obvious fact," he wrote to Tate, which years before had started him on this line of inquiry, was his realization that the requirement of meter in poetry, "an undeniable example of the Formal, does not seem to impair the life and effectiveness of Concrete Experience. They coexist." Here he could well be referring to the speculation which preceded the letter he had written his father fifteen years before. Based upon the summary given in the letter to Tate, in "The Third Moment" Ransom proposed to include many of the critical ideas that in fact did not receive formal expression until the publication of the well-known essays of the thirties, forties, and fifties: that aesthetic theory should have a firm ontological basis; that the material object is the "stuff" of poetry, that the essential nature of poetry resides in its dualism; that the poem can reconstitute the "fugitive first moment," the world's body, through a combination of concept and image; that the view of human experience presented by science, with its practical ends and abstract means, is less than complete; that human experience can be fully realized only through art.

During the 1930s and 40s Ransom made many attempts to define that "precious object," which can restore the concrete particularities of the world's body if one will meditate it properly—that is, if he is impelled "neither to lay hands on the object immediately, nor to ticket it for tomorrow's outrage but to conceive [of] it as having its own existence." To know a work of art one must be capable of an aesthetic experience; he must entertain what Schopenhauer called "knowledge without desire." In the preface to *The World's Body* Ransom indicates that the postscientific poetry to which he and his generation are attached is the "act of a fallen mind," a poetry that attempts to "realize the world," not to "idealize it." Modern man has little knowledge of the world in which he lives except that which is revealed through scientific observation. His conception of the world is faulty because it is incomplete. To view the world only in the manner of the scientist is to fail to realize its body and solid substance. If we are to know the world, "which is made of whole and indefeasible objects," we must recover it through poetry from our memory to which it has retired.[5] Poetry, then, is an order of knowledge quite distinct from that which one achieves through science, and it is the only means through which one can know the concrete particularity of the world's body. This argument is an obvious extension of the line of speculation that Ransom had been engaged in more than ten years before when he tried to identify and define, in the letter to Tate, the "three moments" that comprise the historical order of experience. In his view the only way in which the actual experience can be recovered in its totality is through art, dreams, or religious myth. The record made in the "second moment," by scientists and social scientists, is formed through the process of subtracting from the whole, by formulating concepts and abstract ideas derived from concentration on one aspect of the whole. When man realizes that his record of the experience is only a partial one, he may also understand that the elusive first moment can never be recovered through abstract speculation or philosophical synthesis. If he resorts to poetry as the means through which the experience is reconstituted, he must deal with a mixed world, one composed of both ideas and images.

Ransom's continued interest in this mixed world led him, in some of his most influential essays, to discuss the nature and function of poetry, to differentiate among its several types, and to contrast its

[5] *The World's Body*, p. x.

aims and purposes with those of science. As he covers again this
now very familiar ground, it becomes abundantly clear that there is
no fundamental change in his critical position. What seems a major
shift of belief or opinion is usually an attempt to clarify a misunderstood statement by supplying additional details or, as is often the
case, by changing his metaphor.

In "Poetry: A Note in Ontology" (1934) he defines and ranks
three kinds of poetry. The first is physical poetry, the mode that
the Imagists produced, which intends to "present things in their
thingness," and in this intention is diametrically opposed to "that
poetry which dwells as firmly as it dares upon ideas." The image,
Ransom argues, "cannot be dispossessed of primordial freshness,
which idea can never claim." The image is in its "natural or wild
state," where it has to be discovered; it is not made by man and
operates according to the laws of its own nature. Man cannot "lay
hold of [an] image and take it captive," as he can an idea, which
Ransom defines as the "image with its character beaten out of it."
Science can destroy the image, not as some think—through refu-
tation—but by taming it and destroying its freedom through abstraction. Through the use of the so-called scientific method man
can weaken his imagination to the extent that he can no longer
"contemplate things as they are in their rich and contingent materiality." As he had argued repeatedly over the years in his correspondence with Tate and others, Ransom insists that man is compelled to poetry through memory and dream; it follows, therefore,
that art is "based on second love, not first love." Through it man
attempts to return to something he has lost, to capture that elusive
first moment, the experience itself in all its rich particularity.
Ransom values physical poetry because it attempts to go beyond
the abstractions of science by constant recourse to image, but this
kind of poetry reproduces only a part of the experience. To reconstitute the total experience requires a combination of image
and idea.

If physical poetry is a "half poetry," the second mode, Platonic
poetry, is "bogus poetry." It tries to pose as the real thing by hid-
ing its ideas behind its images, but its images can always be translated into ideas as if to prove that nature is rational and can be
possessed through logic. The Platonic poet does not accept the
basic principle of "the third moment": the world of ideas is not the
original world of perception; therefore the whole and comprehen-
sible object cannot be presented through logical statement. The
original world of perception, the first moment, must be

"experienced, and cannot be reported." Through his false poetry
the Platonist attempts to demonstrate that "an image will prove an
idea," and his images are employed merely as illustrations of ideas.[6]
At this point in the essay Ransom reiterates an argument first
presented many years earlier. Man must "recant from his Platonics
and turn back to things" if he would restore to poetry some of the
vigor and strength that it once possessed; but as he turns from his
idealizing, he must be fully aware of how deeply he has been
affected by his excursion into Platonism. In "Thoughts on the
Poetic Discontent" he had argued that man's mature attitude is
tempered by irony and poetry, because he is reluctant to give up
"the music and color" and the "romantic mystery" of his belief in
the existence of a "mystical community," a union between subject
and object, percept and concept, man and nature.[7] This idea is
restated now in different language. Man's withdrawal from Platonism is neither easy nor complete. From this dualistic state, in
which he is pulled in two directions simultaneously, comes the
complex attitude which produces the aesthetic moment: an instant
of "suspension . . . between the Platonism in us, which is militant,
always sciencing and devouring, and a starved inhibited aspiration
towards innocence" which would like to "know the object as it
might . . . reveal itself." Thus the "poetic impulse is not free." Because it means to reconstitute the world of perception, it stubbornly resists the pressures of science in order to enjoy its images.
From this "adult mode" in which images and ideas vie for the attention of the mature man comes true poetry, and poetry is
produced in that "curious moment of suspension" in which the
imagination attempts to reconstitute an experience which we have
allowed to become mutilated, abstracted, and universalized by the
scientists, the social scientists, and the philosophers.

Out of this "mixed and complex" world comes true poetry. Here
Ransom characterizes this "true poetry" as metaphysical poetry,
although he admitted in a letter to Tate before the essay was
published that the term was too specialized and restrictive. A distinguishing characteristic of this poetry is its use of the conceit,
which Ransom says is a "meant metaphor," one which is
"developed so literally that it must be good" or "predicated so
baldly that nothing else can be meant." In this metaphorical assertion a "miraculism" or "supernaturalism" occurs if the poet not

[6] Ibid., p. 128.
[7] "Thoughts on the Poetic Discontent," *Fugitive*, 4 (1925), 64.

only means what he says but compels the reader to believe what he has read. This miraculism comes as the result of the poet's having discovered "by analogy an identity between objects which is partial, though it should be considerable, and proceeds to an identification which is complete." From this kind of miraculism poetry derives its ontological significance because it makes available an order of knowledge that one can get from no other source. For it is "the poet and nobody else who gives to God a nature, a form, faculties, and a history." Without poetry to give God a body and a solid substance, He "would remain the driest and deadest among Platonic ideas." Myths are "conceits, born of metaphors," and religions are "produced by poets and destroyed by naturalists."[8]

In 1941 Ransom admitted that even after years of dedicated effort he had been unable to find the fusion of thought and feeling that T. S. Eliot had attributed to some of the poets who had lived in the seventeenth century and earlier. He was convinced, he said, that a thought cannot be felt; nevertheless a thought can be and often is conducted simultaneously with "irrelevant feelings." The unique phenomenon which Eliot described can best be presented, Ransom insisted, by what he called his structure-texture formulation, the well-known and often contested phrase he devised to delineate the essential duality of poetry. The reader of a poem, Ransom argues in *The New Criticism* (1941), can realize the *structure*, which is the logical thought, without sacrificing *texture*, which is the free detail, or "the feelings that engage in the free detail." Eliot's affective language can be translated, then, into the objective or cognitive terms which Ransom had developed over twenty-five years. Eliot's "big emotion" is attached to the "main thought" or the "logical structure" of the poem at the same time the "little feelings" are evoked by the "play of the words" or the local texture.

Here Ransom is still attempting to point up the differences between the poetic and the scientific structures, and he insists that this differentiation cannot be made, on the basis of either "moralism," "emotionalism," or "sensibility," for all of these are conducted very well in prose. The unique nature of poetry can be identified only by its odd structure, whose exact purpose is difficult to describe. It is a structure not "so tight and precise on its logical side as a scientific or prose structure usually is" but one that

[8] *The World's Body*, p. 140.

"imparts and carries along a great deal of irrelevant or foreign matter which is clearly not structural but even obstructive." What makes this statement significant is Ransom's insistence that poetry is knowledge because it includes a content which, though of a *kind* similar to that of prose, is of a vastly different *order.* Poetry "treats an order of existence, a grade of objectivity," which cannot be treated in scientific discourse.

The difference between poetry and scientific prose, then, is basically an ontological one; only through poetry can man recover the "body and solid substance of the world." The basic kind of data which science can collect reduces the world to a "scheme of abstract conveniences." Science is interested only in *knowing,* but art has a double function: it wants both to *know* and to *make.* Because their intentions vary so widely, science and art employ different kinds of signs to communicate their discoveries and conclusions: science uses mere symbols whose only function is to refer to some other object, but art uses icons which not only refer to other objects but "resemble or imitate those objects." The object symbolized by the scientific sign is an abstraction or a single property of the object represented, but that suggested by the aesthetic sign or icon is the whole object.[9]

After the publication of "Wanted: An Ontological Critic" in 1941 Ransom wrote many essays in which he attempted to demonstrate how the ontological critic should react in his efforts to define the nature of poetic discourse and to justify its existence in a society becoming more and more enamored of the quasi knowledge and the false promises of science. But as effective as these essays have been in convincing many readers that the truths of poetry can be revealed only through a close and analytical study of the texts itself, they do not represent an essential change in his critical position. Ransom's "restless exploration of the grounds of criticism," to use Allen Tate's phrase, continued, however, and during the forties and fifties he published a dozen or more essays which demonstrate his preoccupation with the unique nature of poetry.[10] In "Poetry: The Formal Analysis" (1947) he castigates some of his fellow critics for concentrating too much on the poem's texture and neglecting its structure. Some of them, he writes, approach the poem in the manner of the "bee who gathers honey

[9]"Wanted: An Ontological Critic," *The New Criticism* (Norfolk, Conn.: New Directions, 1941), pp. 294–336.
[10]"A Note on Critical 'Autotelism,'" *Essays of Four Decades* (Chicago: Swallow, 1970), p. 169.

from the several blossoms as he comes to them, without noticing the bush which supports all the blossoms." Because they are "careless of the theoretical constitution of poetry," these critics tend to create an impression of the poem's disorder at the same time that they make the reader aware of many "exciting turns of poetic language."[11]

In these last essays Ransom covered much of the ground he had been over earlier as he attempts to clear up misunderstood statements or fuzzily expressed concepts. His definition of a poem, however, does not change. Even the language is the same; it remains a "logical structure having a local texture." In "Old Age of an Eagle" he analyzes the three dimensions of a poem: its plot or argument, its meter, and its language.[12] It has an "ostensible argument" which can be rendered in prose and a "tissue of meaning" which cannot. Although a poem is never completely represented in its paraphrase, which always reduces the text, it always includes its own paraphrase, which is both "useful" and "reputable" because it "straightens out the text and prunes meaning down."

In Ransom's three essays on the concrete universal he reiterates his belief that the technical sciences attempt to know the natural world in order to tame it, to reduce it and take what they want from it. Unlike Hegel, who insists that the concrete is wholly assimilated in the universal, he follows Kant in arguing that the "concrete detail is partly extraneous to the abstract universal"; for this reason the complete meaning of a poem can never be expressed in logical terms. Again he attempts to define the unique nature of the poem. His attempt to identify the poem as having a logical structure and an irrelevant texture, he wrote, has worried him because "texture" has come to strike him as "a flat or inadequate figure for that vital and easily felt part of the poem which we associate particularly with poetic language." Now he would say a poem is an "organism," composed of head, heart, and feet.[13] All these organs work together to produce a poem, each speaking in a different language, the head in an intellectual language, the heart in an affective language, and the feet in a rhythmical language. Through appropriate combinations of these three kinds of language, poetry of the right kind can present the concrete universal,

---

[11]"Poetry: The Formal Analysis," *Kenyon Review,* 9 (1947), 436.

[12]*Poems and Essays* (New York: Vintage Books, 1955), p. 79.

[13]"The Concrete Universal: Observations on the Understanding of Poetry," *Kenyon Review,* 16 (1954), 559.

only a part of which is included in the scientific discourse. This kind of poetry can assist the reader in knowing the world, for in it the imagination, through metaphor, makes the moral universal, which is abstract and conceptual, concrete and perceptual. The universal is referred to nature and particularized, given sensuous detail through this reference. Thus nature is essential for poetry. To abandon nature is to abandon metaphor. Without metaphor there can be no poetry, and without poetry man's knowledge of himself and his world is fragmentary and incomplete.

The Pedagogue as Critic

Hugh Kenner

WHAT A CRITIC may hope to accomplish in his lifetime is no more than a few acts of clarification, and if Ransom almost inadvertently accomplished more it is because his unusual powers were aided by a historical opportunity. No man, it is possible to say, has had more effect on the way the subtler operations of language are apprehended in this country in this century. There is probably not a freshman in the United States today whose experience of the English survey—three classroom hours a week plus three more hours of preparing his assignments plus whatever time for term papers his conscience impels or his roommate permits—is not in large part traceable to concerns of Ransom's. It makes no difference that he has never heard of Ransom. For that matter the teaching assistant in charge of the section has himself only just possibly heard of Ransom, and has almost certainly given him no thought. (With his own dissertation to worry about, such thought would be a luxury.) The teaching and the learning operate in a kind of determining climate to which explicit attention need not be given; and if I seem to be crediting Ransom with magical powers, as though by lifting his finger, or by writing a few books that hardly anyone bought, he had managed to create a durable anticyclone, let me specify that I am concerned with a sort of mythical over-view, as our only hope of encompassing our subject within the given space. Ransom's biographer will occupy himself with the de-tailed intricacies. All I propose to do is furnish the biographer with a statement of one of his necessary themes, and ourselves with a lit-tle whole-system understanding.

The scope of the Whole System in question is not poetic but pedagogic. That seems a scandalous truth and is often dodged; which of us does not suspect that pedagogic method touches on America's dreariest vulgarities? But dodging it leaves unanswerable such questions as what the New Criticism may have been and what happened to it. There seem to be no New Critics in business today, and if they are judged as extinct as the wild pigeon or the dodo, that may be because surly folk clubbed them all to death, or be-cause they go disguised as old critics now. More likely they are extinct for the same reason that the unicorn is extinct. Expeditions find no unicorns because none have existed. It is arguable that the New Critic in the same way was always a genteel fiction. His art had little to do with literary criticism but much to do with the teaching of literature, and teaching is the most evanescent of performances, unless we count skydiving, than which however teaching makes more difference to the nonpractitioners.

The importance of the teacher—particularly the college teacher—in the American scheme of things cannot be overestimated. If we want some quantitative measure we may reflect that some 40 percent of the young Americans of an age to attend some institution of "higher learning" do in fact attend one. No effort has been made anywhere in history to detain so many people in classrooms for so many years, and if it is proposed that not a great deal of learning goes on, it may be countered that the tacit point is not really the learning of skills and subjects, in which it is true that the average grade is C. What gets learned is a common language, at a level of abstraction that grades cannot touch. At that level we may describe a language as a body of inarticulate shared assumptions; no one makes grammatical errors, and eloquence of performance, in fact performance itself, is not at issue. This does not sound much like language as most of us understand language, and yet it is the most powerful set of vectors in the language field: the invisible tensile network that holds the words together, as gravitation, invisible likewise, holds the mere objects in the solar system together, setting limits within which they move with seeming freedom.

To call this nonverbal cohesiveness an aspect of language is especially appropriate in America, so much importance have Americans from the outset accorded to sequences of words and to the very act of uttering and naming. William Carlos Williams more than once reflected on the fatefulness of the decision, centuries ago, to name a certain orange-feathered bird a robin, after a different bird remembered from England. Like the cities the colonists called New Amsterdam and New London, the birds they chose to call robins could be stripped of alien identity and transformed into tokens of a continuity for which men hungered. Symptoms of the alien, by nothing more than a name, had been conjured out of existence: for better or worse. (Williams thought it a fateful act of self-deception.)

Then the nation declared its novel identity by means of a declaration and a written constitution: two historical documents, but also two pieces of canonical prose, to be examined and memorized. To their number President Lincoln was to add the Gettysburg Address. American schoolchildren read the address intact, and study it sentence by sentence. We should reflect on the oddity of this fact. England's history has occasioned no such canonical writing, with the complex exception of the King James Bible. It abounds in consecrated gestures: Cromwell saying, "Take away that bauble"; Victoria affirming her nonamusement. What this connoisseurship of theatrical moments may have to do with the fact that England's principal author was a man of the theater would be a theme for a different inquiry. Suffice it to say that it is America, where the national prose is allegedly barbarous, that makes a cult of connected pieces of prose writing; and it is England, where men of no other discernible credentials can generate fluent five-thousand-word book reviews, that can hardly scrape up three consecutive sentences anyone can remember.

It was into this highly language-conscious milieu that pedagogy in the nineteenth century introduced the classroom study of English literature. Acquaintance with a range of vernacular literature had become a synonym for being cultivated. But fiction and poetry written in another country could scarcely be expected to have other than a classroom existence, and that is the kind of existence literature in America has tended to have. Even among nonprofessional people with leisure, which in America until recently meant chiefly ladies with servants, it has tended to be something to *study*. But the American classroom is like no other: not only the place where rudiments are inculcated, "for the instruction" (as Jefferson put it) "of those who will come after us," but the place where that which is taught chiefly exists: where a considerable part of the nation's mental life is actually conducted.

Imagine, then, the translation into an American classroom of a poem by John Keats:

> Season of mists and mellow fruitfulness,
>   Close bosom-friend of the maturing sun;
> Conspiring with him how to load and bless
>   With fruit the vines that round the thatch-eaves run;

Move that into Idaho and mark how it is orphaned. It enters the New World naked, cold, uncertain of all save that it enters. How bound up it is, first of all, with an alien weather. American autumns are not misty but crisp. California students stare numbly at that word *mists* and puzzle over the import of *mellow*. Neither word ac-

cords with any experience that they have had of the month of
October (when it does not rain in Southern California) or
November (when it may, and between rains the skies are fiercely
clear). And "thatch-eaves": a Disneyland décor. And those home-
grown vines in the eaves; and that biblical locution *bless with
fruit*—these touch on areas of vague feeling where Bible Chris-
tianity interacts with a lifelong experience of not trusting the
weather, so that weeks of beneficent weather are remarkable and
call for an ode. Keats goes on: "To bend with apples the moss'd
cottage-trees. . . ." Mossed because old, because weathered by
centuries of damp; cherished by cottagers; and a cottage something other than a vacation retreat, rather a humble, substantial
shelter for generations of immovable folk. It is like deciphering the
Greek of Sappho, and wondering what flowers exactly were before
her mind, in those unforgettable catalogues of flowers.

It is worth a real effort to conceive how desperately philological
is the effort to Americanize something like that, because if we can
begin to glimpse the difficulties we can see how inevitable were the
strategies that got employed. One was a natural one for young
readers: the biographical. Its gambit, since the poem would not at-
tach itself readily to the students' experience of autumn, was to at-
tach it to their experience of being alive and young and having feelings. Keats was an impassioned young man whose time was short.
"To Autumn" was one precipitate of his soul's obscure but
vigorous chemistry. He *felt* like that. (You can't argue with a feeling.) Professionalize this tactic, and when you are in graduate
school you will be giving your attention to Keats's letters, among
which his poems will take their place as documents, on the whole
less penetrable than the letters are.

Another strategy, suitable for more mature students whose attention spans may be judged rather long, is to place the poem in
some historical process which it will serve to illustrate. An ideal history for this purpose is that of romanticism, which one can
decorate, if it seems unsuitably abstract, with remarks about "na-
ture-feeling." Apples on mossed cottage-trees are assuredly part of
Nature, and for Nature it is good to have feelings.

Then there is the Moral Strategy, apt to dwell upon final words:
"And gathering swallows twitter in the skies." They gather to depart, and twitter in calling attention to this fact. Here is the
teacher's cue to devise a peroration about the worth of feelings of
composure. The poet composes the transience of autumn fruition
into his celebration of its fructiveness: seeing steadily and whole.

This strategy works better with "Ode on a Grecian Urn," which makes some kind of philosophical statement just as it is ending, and so fits the paradigms we learned from McGuffey's reader, which McGuffey himself would have learned in classrooms where Horace was the approved schoolmaster-poet, assuring unruly boys that the prudent course is after all the middle course.

To assimilate an English poem—it is the story of the robin over again. As men newly arrived from England drew security from mis-naming an unfamiliar bird, so later people long resident in the new world did violence—could not but do violence—to English writing (so much of which is, after all, indifferently written—can anyone feel sure he remembers exactly the words in which Oliver Twist asks for more? The Theatrical Moment again, masquerading as literature). And those modes of violence were institutionalized; that is a short history of the North American English department, up to about 1945: "the old brass-bound English department," Cleanth Brooks used to say, referring to an impressive mindless curiosity like a Victorian railway train. What had begun as a set of strategic necessities had turned into a profession, a way of life, and a stultifying of literary sensibility. The methods of the Germanic seminar made matters worse by equipping mindlessness with the pretentions of method.

Paradise Lost, though equipped with a fierce headnote concerning "that which hath stumbled many, why the Poem Rimes not," contains here and there extraordinary effects of rhyme. Forty years ago a scholar counted and classified them. He listed as many adjacent rhymed lines as could be found: couplets, so to speak. Then he went through the poem carefully again, pausing at the end of each line to see whether the next line but one chanced to end with the same sound, and so made a table of rhymes separated by an unrhymed line. He next repeated this process, sitting, one must suppose, late at night after students and deans were asleep and the college cat put out, placing his finger on a terminal word, sounding this word so as not to be confused by orthography, and checking it against the sound of the terminal word three lines away. This yielded a table of rhymes separated by two unrhymed lines. I do not remember whether he returned to page one and commenced tabulating the rhymes separated by three unrhymed lines, but I know that you can find his results in the bound volumes of *PMLA*, attended by no sign of curiosity whatever as to whether Milton may have admitted these rhymes in the service of any purpose, or for that matter which ones it is even possible for the normally attentive ear to hear as rhymes. And of such, in that prewar decade, was the kingdom of Heaven.

(In passing, I should supply a perspective for such antics by contrasting them with human playfulness. I once heard the British painter and writer Michael Ayrton assert that of all Shakespeare's sonnets only the one commencing "Shall I compare thee to a summer's day" makes consecutive sense if you read its lines in reverse order, beginning with line 14 and ending with line 1. On being asked how on earth he knew this, he replied that in Essex one had to get through the long winter evenings somehow. This rhymes with the British passion for impenetrable crossword puzzles, and has the interesting result of throwing some light on Shakespeare's syntactic habits. It is not to be recommended as a method of research.)

It was in the 1930s, the decade in which Milton's rhymes were counted, that Mr. Ransom began to be heard from. By 1938 there had come into existence a textbook called *Understanding Poetry*, of which he did not write a line apart from some of the verse it anthologized, but which, following our mythological method, we may nearly say he composed throughout without touching pen to paper. I am here, for simplicity's sake, resorting to a Ransom myth, much as classical scholars, after the *Iliad* had been disintegrated into an assemblage of lays by numerous hands, used to employ the Homeric Myth. If you went on talking as though there had been but one author it made for simpler sentences at least, and in sweeping together beneath one name the accomplishments of numerous men associated with Ransom, sometimes remotely associated—in availing myself of that convenient fiction the New Criticism, which hardly anyone would admit to really practicing and which Ransom for his part perhaps did no more than give a name to, I am not only simplifying my sentences but remembering that my subject is the Pedagogue as Critic, amid constant reminders of how American is the figure such a critic cuts.

What the New Criticism did was return the study of literature—of poetry, primarily—to the central American intellectual concern, which is Language.

It looked, in those days, like a New Scholasticism for Poloniuses to shake their heads over after the prince had averred that what he read was words, words, words. We began to hear of wit and irony, of paradox and tension. Whole chains of imagery interacted, in likeness and in difference. Fanny Brawne's name went unmentioned, and Shakespeare's deer-stealing. Dates were omitted.

Spellings were modernized, and one was encouraged to read seventeenth-century words as though they had been written yesterday—

> I wonder, by my troth, what thou and I
> Did, till we lov'd?

and words written nearly yesterday as though all the time since
Shakespeare had hallowed them—

> Here I am, an old man in a dry month,
> Being read to by a boy, waiting for rain.

The Poem Itself—that was what the New Criticism purported to
be about.

About the New Criticism Itself, now that we have worked our
way up to it, I want to make several interrelated observations. The
first is that in treating the poem as a verbal artifact the New
Criticism reached deep into the American linguistic sensibility.
William Carlos Williams in 1945 had called the poem "a small—or
large—machine made out of words," and that was how the New
Critics also thought of the poem, though as good agrarians they
avoided the word *machine*. Such a sense of things is intimate with
the American Grain. It was an American, Edgar Allan Poe, who
spun out an outrageous theory postulating that the last thing for a
poet to bring to mind, after he has his form and his rhymes and
some of his words, may be his subject. He is making a verbal clock-
work which appropriates some subject. It was an American linguist,
Benjamin Lee Whorf, who elaborated a theory that our language
does not report but creates our simplest perceptions, as though we
all lived inside a collective poem. Again it is the words that come
first. More recently it was an American engineer, Claude E. Shannon, who devised information theory, which has us attend not to
the speaker but to the system of encoding. (Ransom's comments on
how his own poems were changed by his revisions direct our attention in a similar way.)

Neither for Poe nor for Whorf nor for Shannon does language
proceed from a human interior, though we can reconstruct a
human intention from it if we are skilled. The New Critic in the
same way warned us not to mistake the poem for an utterance of
the poet, and an intricate terminology of "speaker" and "per-
sona"—not Keats or Donne but "Keats" and "Donne," each in the
role that he plays on this occasion—admonished readers that
biography was irrelevant and that all there was to know of the poet
in connection with this poem was what this poem could be

persuaded to yield. This entailed the formulation whereby all poetry is dramatic, with the incidental advantages both of incorporating Shakespeare's prestige and of coping with the fact that the life of so great a poet has so little to offer us.

My second and third observations are interrelated: that the New Critical thrust was toward facilitating classroom discussion, and that its procedures tended to move into prominence chiefly those poets whom they rendered lengthily discussable. Hence the odd paradox that Williams, despite his dictum about the word-machine, was almost totally neglected. This neglect proceeded from no bias against modernity, since part of the benefit of these novel preoccupations was supposed to be the quantity of contemporary work that they made accessible. Moreover by concentrating on the chemistries of language you could draw comparable satisfactions from poets who made "statements" and from poets who didn't, unembarrassed by the absence of summarizing sentences. *The Waste Land*—not a favorite of Ransom's by the way—became a young critic's obstacle course, through which he was expected to scramble beneath a hail of live ammunition from the battlements of brassboundery, before being adjudged fit for intelligence work. No, the difficulty was that when disassembled by the approved methods, the Williams machine was insufficiently complicated. Not even "The Crimson Cyclamen"—as close a thing, I would argue, to a metaphysical poem as we have in modern English—lends itself to the isolation of "tensions" and "paradoxes" that are effective in the classroom and lend themselves well to the blackboard. And as for "The Red Wheelbarrow," what do you put on the board after you have put the sixteen words of the poem on the board?

Which permits me to elide into my fourth observation, that in subjecting the words on the page to their famous scrutiny, the New Critics tended to scrutinize rather than to listen. A typical blackboard at the end of the hour would display words encircled, with little colliding arrows; would show lines broken into phrases, with perhaps some stresses marked; and would generally be faithful to the discussion of which it carried the traces, since a blackboard permits no interest in what lines sound like, and generally the classes didn't either.[1] It was perhaps as part of the ritual exorcism of

[1] The National Endowment for the Humanities might stockpile precious material for twenty-first–century cultural historians by endowing for six months a team to walk through classrooms at the end of each academic day and photograph blackboards.

Tennyson, "mouthing out his hollow oes and aes," that this order
of omission was tolerated; partly too it stemmed from a certain fear
of vulgarity—sound can *impose*—and partly from the persistent
though usually unspecified metaphor of the artifact: the precision
machine, the well-wrought urn. The persistent neglect of Pound
throughout the new critical years was sometimes excused by the
allegation—I once heard Cleanth Brooks make it—that Pound
never made a poem that was a finished whole. But Pound's poems
are apt to be completed—not merely enhanced—by their metrical
and vocalic components,[2] so we have here an instance of the field
of interest being diminished by critical preoccupations. (And it was
Donne, who Ben Jonson thought "for not keeping of accent de-
served hanging," who was apt to be deemed the poet par ex-
cellence.)

The cult of the blackboard sponsored other distortions: early
Yeats underrated, late Yeats sometimes overrated; Wallace
Stevens's work unsorted into the categories it demands, the live
parts distinguished from the parts that are rhythmically dead. An
indifference persisted, for that matter, to rhythmic deadness in
modern after modern, just so sufficient surface complication was
discoverable.

My purpose behind this catalogue of omissions and distortions is
not to denigrate the critic-pedagogue, but to define his characteristic limits of activity, by way of defining what he can do
superlatively well, and why, in the 1940s and 1950s, it mattered so
much.

What he does is trace the play of mind through a poem, in a way
that depends as little as possible on knowledge the students won't
have and shouldn't be distracted by. All that is in front of the naive
student is the poem, and every minute that is spent on the
biography of Yeats or the topography of Sligo is a minute during
which his capacity for getting interested in the poem will dissipate
by several quanta. A half-hour spent on the doctrines of
romanticism insures that meanwhile a dozen odes will die in their
entirety. Any strategy for entering directly into the text, and en-
countering the strange capacity of its words for engaging one
another and absorbing attention, is clearly preferable to a pedagogic habit that lingers amid peripheral data, because in no other
way can the life of the poem be saved, the life that alone confers

[2] See, in *The Pound Era* (Berkeley and Los Angeles: University of California
Press, 1971), my discussions of "The Return" (pp. 189–91) and of Canto LXXXI
(pp. 488–93).

interest on other orders of lore. (What interest whatever can romanticism possibly have, unless we first find some romantic poems interesting? Unless they interest the mind to the point where the mind possesses them, they simply are not "there," and without the poems the movement isn't "there" either, and time spent on its study is spent on precisely nothing.)

The curious thing is how a classroom strategy could come to mistake itself for a critical discipline. Not to distract students with peripheral information, that is one thing; to pretend to oneself, as some New Critics did, that the information has no status whatever, is something else. It is possible at all because poems are very tough, viable in strange environments, even in the zero environment of absolute ahistoricity, with only the circulatory system of Language itself to nourish them. How they can protect their existence by mutation is a theme that deserves more attention than it has received. Shakespeare's "golden lads," for instance, has exerted power over countless imaginations despite the virtual loss of the information that what he wrote down was a Warwickshire idiom for dandelions.[3] And Ransom's influential discussion of "Lycidas" ("A Poem Nearly Anonymous") illuminates the poem despite the demonstrable inaccuracy of its postulate—that Milton "roughened" a poem he had first written "smooth." Despite missing information, misinformation, even downright wrong information, it is possible for discussion to proceed a long way without losing itself in nonsense. We may hope to see the way of this elucidated, as information (we may also hope) works itself (duly subordinated) back into our classrooms.

There is no way of not emphasizing classrooms. Criticism is nothing but explicit reading, reading articulating its themes and processes in the presence of more minds than one. It is natural for more minds than one to be concerned, because it is natural to want to talk about what interests one, and also because language itself can only exist at the focus of many minds. And it is in the classroom that, for better or worse, this process of shared and explicit reading is destined to localize itself. (The Browning study groups are, thank heaven, dead.)

What is important is that the very terms on which poems exist shall not surrender once more to the exactions of the beginning student. More than twenty years ago Walter J. Ong described a whole department of human thought, the "arts-course scholas-

---

[3] For this and other examples see *The Pound Era*, pp. 121–26.

ticism" of the late Middle Ages, as having been shaped almost
wholly by the need to devise a "philosophy" that could be taught
to bright adolescents.[4] It existed only in classrooms, and prepared
the minds that, both by penetration and by reaction, prepared the
renaissance. By analogy we may call the New Criticism the
scholastic phase of an American poetic, rescuing poetics in the New
World both from naiveté and from disappearance by absorption
into other subjects such as psychology and history.

That, we may say, is accomplished; at least that. In the decades
ahead we shall see what we shall see.

[4]"Ramus: Rhetoric and the Pre-Newtonian Mind," *English Institute Essays
1952* (New York: Columbia University Press, 1954), pp. 138–70; see esp. pp.
161–63.

The Linguistic Moment
in "The Wreck of the Deutschland"

J. Hillis Miller

BY LINGUISTIC MOMENT I mean the moment when language as such, the means of representation in literature, becomes a matter to be interrogated, explored, thematized in itself. Such questioning may seem a special feature of literary criticism today, but in fact it has always been present in one way or another in literature itself. It may be that, in our tradition at least, literature is to be distinguished from other uses of language by its momentum toward such self-questioning, rather than by specific ethical or metaphysical themes. In any case, in the work of some writers among the Victorians, in spite of their overt commitment to a mimetic theory of literature, this linguistic moment becomes explicit enough and prolonged enough so that it displaces nature or human nature as the primary focus of imaginative activity. Examples would include the work of Meredith, of Ruskin, or of Pater.[1]

A similar displacement from nature, from the self, and even from God may be observed in the poetic thought of Gerard Manley Hopkins. As I have elsewhere argued and as is easy to see, there are in fact three apparently incompatible theories of poetry in Hopkins, each brilliantly worked out in theory and exemplified in practice.[2] Poetry may be the representation of the interlocked chiming of created things in their relation to the Creation. This chiming makes the pied beauty of nature. Poetry may explore or express the solitary adventures of the self in its wrestles with God or in its fall into the abyss outside God.[3] Poetry may explore the intri-

[1] I have borrowed in this introductory paragraph some sentences and phrases from a forthcoming paper entitled "The Linguistic Moment: Nature, Self, and Language in the Victorians." In this essay I have tried as best I can to honor the example of John Crowe Ransom's criticism.

[2] In the essay on Hopkins in *The Disappearance of God* (Cambridge: Harvard University Press, Belknap Press, 1963), pp. 270–359.

[3] Compare the admirable passage in Hopkins's commentary on *The Spiritual Exercises* of Saint Ignatius: "And this [my isolation] is much more true when we consider the mind; when I consider my selfbeing, my consciousness and feeling of myself, that taste of myself, of *I* and *me* above and in all things, which is more distinctive than the taste of ale or alum, more distinctive than the smell of walnutleaf or camphor, and is incommunicable by any means to another man"

cate relationships among words. These three seemingly diverse
theories of poetry are harmonized by the application to all of them
of a linguistic model. This model is based on the idea that all words
rhyme because they are ultimately derived from the same Logos.
Nature is "word, expression, news of God" (*Sermons*, p. 129), and
God has inscribed himself in nature. The structure of nature in its
relation to God is like the structure of language in relation to the
Logos, the divine Word; and Christ is the Logos of nature, as of
words. The permutations of language, as in the final two lines of
"That Nature Is a Heraclitean Fire," correspond to or mime the
permutations of the self as it is changed by grace from its Jackself,
steeped in sin, turned from God, to a more Christ-like, Logosimilar,
self:

> I am all at once what Christ is,   since he was what I am, and
> This Jack, joke, poor potsherd,   patch, matchwood, immortal
>   diamond,
>   Is immortal diamond.

> [*Poems*, p. 106]

   In all three realms the notion of rhyme, or the echoing at a
distance of entities which are similar without being identical, is
essential. Since the structure of language is the indispensable
model or metaphor by means of which Hopkins describes nature or
the self, the actual nature of language is a matter of fundamental
importance to him. From the earliest writings of his (aside from ju-
venile letters) that are extant, the "Early Diaries," to the last
poems, Hopkins shows his fascination with language as such. It is
one theme of his masterwork, the poem which combines latently
all the later poetry, both the poetry of nature and the poetry of the
self—"The Wreck of the Deutschland." Language is not just ad-
mirably exploited by Hopkins in "The Wreck" to say what he

(Christopher Devlin, ed., *The Sermons and Devotional Writings of Gerard
Manley Hopkins* [London: Oxford University Press, 1959], p. 123; hereafter cited
as *Sermons*). Citations from other titles by Hopkins will be identified as follows:
Journals is Humphry House and Graham Storey, eds., *The Journals and Papers of
Gerard Manley Hopkins* (London: Oxford University Press, 1959); *Poems* is W. H.
Gardner and N. H. MacKenzie, eds., *The Poems of Gerard Manley Hopkins*, 4th
ed. rev. (London: Oxford University Press, 1967); *Letters 2* is Claude Colleer Ab-
bot, ed., *The Correspondence of Gerard Manley Hopkins and Richard Watson
Dixon* (London: Oxford University Press, 1955); *Letters 3* is Claude Colleer Ab-
bott, ed., *Further Letters of Gerard Manley Hopkins*, 2d ed. (London: Oxford
University Press, 1956). Line numbers shown parenthetically after quotations
refer to "The Wreck of the Deutschland."

wants to say. It is also interrogated for its own sake. One can see why, since everything else, his vision of nature and the self in their relations to God, hangs on the question of the nature of language and of the adequacy of the linguistic metaphor.

Everywhere in "The Wreck of the Deutschland" may be seen operating as its fundamental organizing principle the exploitation of rhyme in an extended sense—that is, as the echoing at a distance of elements which are similar without being identical. Rhyme operates in "The Wreck" both on the microscopic level of local poetical effect and on the macroscopic level of the large structural repetitions organizing the whole.

On the local level there are repetitions with a difference of word sounds, of word meanings, and of rhythmical patterns. As is indicated by the etymological speculations in Hopkins's early diaries, the basis of Hopkins's interest in the labyrinth of relations among the sounds of words is the assumption that if words sound the same they will be similar in meaning. Each sequence of words with the same consonant pattern but with different vowels—for example, *flick, fleck, flake,*—is assumed to be a variation on a single ur-meaning from which they are all derived. But all words whatsoever, all permutations of all the letters of the alphabet, are assumed to have a common source in the Word, "him that present and past, / Heaven and earth are word of, worded by," as Hopkins puts it in this poem (ll. 229–30). This attention to sound similarities in their relation to similarities of meaning is perhaps most apparent in the emphatic use of alliteration throughout the poem (breath / bread, strand / sway / sea, bound / bones in the first few lines); but there are many other forms of sound echo—assonance, end rhyme, internal rhyme, recurrences of vowel sequences, and so on—which the attentive reader will follow as threads of embodied meaning in the tapestry of the poem. In all these cases the underlying assumption is theological as well as technical. The fact that Christ is the Word, or Logos, of which all particular words are versions, variations, or metaphors allows Hopkins even to accommodate deliberately into his poem words which are similar in sound though opposite in meaning. Christ underlies all words and thereby reconciles all oppositions in word sound and meaning: "Thou art lightning and love, I found it, a winter and warm" (l. 70).

The same assumptions are the grounds for the various forms of repetition with a difference of word meaning in the poem. The complex fabric of recurring metaphors is not mere verbal play to unify the poem. This fabric is based on the assumption that meta-

phorical comparisons reflect ontological correspondences in the
world, correspondences placed there by the God whom heaven
and earth are word of, worded by. Fire, water, sand, and wind are
the primary elements of this "metaphorology." To the recurrence
of metaphors may be added the repetition of metaphorical elements by thematic motifs which exist on the literal level of narrative in the poem. It is no accident that the poet's experience of
grace in the first part of the poem is described in terms of fire, sand,
and water which anticipate the elements literally present in the
lightning, sandbar, and ocean waves of the "The Wreck."

In the same way Hopkins's frequent use of puns assumes that a
single sound may be a meeting place, crossroads, or verbal "knot"
where several distinct verbal strands converge. This convergence is
once more evidence of ontological relations among the various
meanings present in layers in a single word. Man's condition as
sullenly fallen, stubbornly "tied to his turn" away from God ("Rib-
blesdale," l. 11), for example, may be expressed by calling him
"dogged in den" (l. 67). Here "dogged" is a quadruple pun meaning sullenly determined, doglike, twisted down (as a "dog" is a
kind of bolt), and hounded (as a wild animal is chased by dogs into
its den and kept at bay there). There may also be an expression of
the reciprocal or mirror-image relation between man and God in
the fact that dog, man's epithet here, reverses the letters that spell
God. This would give a fifth level of implication to the pun.

Hopkins's use of sprung rhythm, a distinctive feature of "The
Wreck of the Deutschland," is discussed briefly in the well-known
letter of October 5, 1878, to R. W. Dixon. Hopkins's prosodic
practice is a complex matter, since most of his verse combines
sprung rhythm with elements from the ordinary accentual rhythm
of English poetry; but the basic principle of sprung rhythm is
simple enough. Each foot or measure has a single strong beat, but
there may be "any number of weak or slack syllables" (Author's
Preface, *Poems*, p. 47), so that a foot may have only one syllable or
many, though the time length of all feet is the same. This gives the
great effect of tension or "springing" to such verse. Moreover it
should be remembered that Hopkins insisted that sprung rhythm is
the "rhythm of common speech and of written prose, when
rhythm is perceived in them" (Author's Preface, p. 49). Hopkins
expected his poetry to be recited aloud with the emphases and
rhythms of common speech. A valuable note written apropos of
"The Wreck of the Deutschland" makes explicit the way Hopkins
wanted the poem to be recited:

Be pleased, reader, since the rhythm in which the following poem is written is new, strongly to mark the beats of the measure, according to the number belonging to each of the eight lines of the stanza, as the indentation guides the eye, namely two and three and four and three and five and five and four and six; not disguising the rhythm and rhyme, as some readers do, who treat poetry as if it were prose fantastically written to rule (which they mistakenly think the perfection of reading), but laying on the beats too much stress rather than too little; nor caring whether one, two, three, or more syllables go to a beat, that is to say, whether two or more beats follow running—as there are three running in the third line of the first stanza—or with syllables between, as commonly, nor whether the line begin with a beat or not; but letting the scansion run on from one line into the next, without break to the end of the stanza: since the dividing of the lines is more to fix the places of the necessary rhymes than for any pause in the measure. . . . And so throughout let the stress be made to fetch out both the strength of the syllables and the meaning and feeling of the words. (*Poems*, pp. 255–256)

The rhythmical complexities in "The Wreck" are not, however, merely experimental ends in themselves. They are another form of repetition with variation, another way to set down or to specify a given sound pattern which is then differentially echoed in later units of the poem, according to the fundamental principle of all poetry, which Hopkins identified in "Poetry and Verse" (1873 or 1874) as "repetition, *oftening, over-and-overing, aftering*" (*Journals*, p. 289).

Finally the sprung rhythm of "The Wreck" has as much a theological basis as any of the other forms of rhyme. As Hopkins says in the letter to Dixon of 1878, he "had long had haunting [his] ear the echo of a new rhythm which now [he] realized on paper" (*Letters*, 2:14). The strategic use of the metaphor of music in "The Wreck" makes it clear that the rhythm echoed in the poet's ear and then embodied in the words of the poem is no less than the fundamental rhythm or groundswell of the creation, the ratio, measure, or Logos which pervades all things as a fundamental melody may be varied or echoed throughout a great symphony. The long Platonic and Christian tradition connecting the notion of rhythm to the Logos or underlying principle of things, "Ground of being, and granite of it" (l. 254), as Hopkins calls it here, is subtly integrated into the texture of thought of this poem as well as into its rhythmical practice. When the poet is at the point of affirming attunement of the tall nun with the name of Christ, worded everywhere in the creation, he affirms that His name is "her mind's" "measure" and "burden" (ll. 215, 216), where "measure" is musical measure and "burden" is fundamental melody, as in Shakespeare's "Come Unto these Yellow Sands": "And, sweet sprites, the burden bear." The sprung rhythm of "The Wreck" is not merely a device for achieving a high degree of tension and patterning in the poem but is based on the belief that God himself is a rhythm which the poet may echo in his verse, his breath in its modulations and tempo answering God's "arch and original Breath" (l. 194).

To these small-scale forms of organization corresponds the way in which the large-scale dramatic or narrative structure of the poem is put together. Like "Lycidas," "Adonais," or *In Memoriam* "The Wreck of the Deutschland" is only nominally about the dead whom it memorializes. The poet's response to the death of another is the occasion for a highly personal poem about the poet's inner life and his sense of vocation. Once again repetition with variation is the basis of Hopkins's poetic practice.

The key to the overall structure of "The Wreck of the Deutschland" is given in stanza eighteen in which the poet describes his tears when he reads of the death of the nuns in his safe haven "away in the loveable west, / On a pastoral forehead of Wales" (ll. 185–186): "Why, tears! is it? tears; such a melting, a madrigal start!" (l. 142). The poet's tears are a madrigal echo or rhyme of the nun's suffering—that is, an echo of the same melody on a different pitch, as in the basic musical structure of a Renaissance madrigal, canon, or round. This canonlike response leads the poet first to reenact in memory an earlier experience in which he felt God's grace, then, in the second part of the poem, to reenact in his imagination the death of the nuns. The doubling of this narrative, the memory of his own experience doubling his vivid picture of the shipwreck, causes a redoubling in a new experience of God's presence to the poet. This new experience of grace occurs within the poem itself and is in fact identical with the writing of it. The poem is addressed directly to God in the present tense, and this immediate relation of reciprocity between the poet and the God who "masters" him is the "now" of the poem generated by its doubling and redoubling of the two earlier "nows" which it reiterates.

All the various techniques of "rhyme" in "The Wreck of the Deutschland," though perhaps based on methods Hopkins had learned from Pindar's odes, from Old English verse, or from the complex Welsh system of poetry called *cynghanedd*, are in fact a magnificent exploitation of the general properties of language as they may be put to the specifically poetic use. This use Roman

Jakobson calls the set of language towards itself.[4] This formulation occurs in an essay in which Jakobson quotes with approval Hopkins's expression of the same idea. In the passage in question Hopkins defines poetry as repetition. As he puts it, "poetry is in fact speech only employed to carry the inscape of speech for the inscape's sake," and "in this light poetry is speech which afters and oftens its inscape, speech couched in a repeating figure" (*Journals*, p. 289).

Hopkins's exploitation of the multiple possibilities of repetition in language is, however, based throughout on the theological notion that God is the Word. The divine Word is the basis of all words in their relations of similarity and difference. The play of phonic, verbal, and rhythmical texture in "The Wreck of the Deutschland" is controlled by the fixed idea of a creator, God, who has differentiated himself in the creation. The world is full of things which echo one another and rhyme. The same God is also the Word behind all words, the "arch and original Breath." The branches and twigs of the tree of language are divided in derived forms of the initial Word. Word and world in this happily correspond because they have the same source.

This theory of poetic language is not merely exploited in "The Wreck." It is one of the chief thematic strands in the poem. Repeatedly, in one way or another throughout "The Wreck," the question of language comes up, for example in "I did say yes" and "truer than tongue" in the second stanza (ll. 9, 11). One main theme of the poem is its own possibility of being. "The Wreck of the Deutschland," like many great poems of the nineteenth and twentieth centuries, is, in part at least, about poetry. In this, in spite of Hopkins's Catholicism, he may be seen as a poet in the romantic tradition, a poet who belongs in the great line leading from Wordsworth, Blake, and Hölderlin through Baudelaire, Tennyson, and Rimbaud to poets of our own century like Yeats, Rilke, and Stevens. Moreover, by exploring this aspect of the poem, the reader encounters what is most problematic about it, both in its form and in its meaning.

In a celebrated letter to Baillie of January 14, 1883, Hopkins develops a theory that in classical literature (for example in Greek tragedy) the overt narrative meaning may be matched by a covert

---

[4] In Roman Jakobson, "Concluding Statement: Linguistics and Poetics," *Style in Language*, ed. Thomas A. Sebeok (Cambridge, Mass.: The M.I.T. Press, 1960), p. 356: "The set (*Einstellung*) toward the MESSAGE as such, focus on the message for its own sake, is the POETIC function of language."

sequence of figures or allusions constituting what he calls an "underthought." This will be an "echo or shadow of the over-thought . . . an undercurrent of thought governing the choice of images used." "My thought," says Hopkins, "is that in any lyric passage of the tragic poets . . . there are—usually; I will not say al-ways, it is not likely—two strains of thought running together and like counterpointed; the overthought that which everybody, editors, see . . . and which might for instance be abridged or paraphrased . . . the other, the underthought, conveyed chiefly in the choice of metaphors etc used and often only half realized by the poet himself. . . . The underthought is commonly an echo or shadow of the overthought, something like canons and repetitions in music, treated in a different manner" (*Letters*, 3:252–253). If the overthought of "The Wreck of the Deutschland" is the story of the tall nun's salvation and its musical echo both before and after by the poet's parallel experience of grace, the underthought of the poem is its constant covert attention to problems of language. This linguistic theme is in a subversive relation of counterpoint to the theological overthought.

One important thematic element in "The Wreck of the Deutsch-land" is the image of a strand, rope, finger, vein, or stem. This image is Hopkins's way of expressing the link between creator and created. One form of this motif, however, is precisely "tongue," present in the poem in "truer than tongue" (l. 11), in "past telling of tongue" (l. 69), with its reference to the gift of tongues which descended at Pentecost on the Apostle in tongues of flame (Acts, 2:1 ff.), in "a virginal tongue told" (l. 136), and in the conflation of God's finger and the tongue of the bell which the tall nun rings (stanza 31). The creative stem of stress between God and his crea-tures is also a tongue that speaks by modulating the archoriginal breath, the undifferentiated word which is Christ, as the tongues of fire at Pentecost were "cloven."

Christ, the second person of the Trinity, the link between God the father and the creation, is both a principle of unity, the only means by which man may return to the singleness of the Godhead, and at the same time He is the principle of differentiation. Christ is the model for the multiplicity of individual things in the world, including that most highly individuated creature, man. This is one meaning justifying Hopkins's epithet for Christ in stanza thirty-four: "double-naturèd name" (l. 266). Christ is both God and man, both one and many. If he is the avenue by which man loses his indi-viduality in God, in imitating Christ or, like the tall nun, in reading

Christ as the single word of the creation, at the same time Christ is
the basis of puns in language. He is also the explanation of the fact
that God manifests himself as both lightning and love, as winter
and warm—that is, in words that sound alike but have opposite
meanings. The devil is in this a diabolical imitation of Christ, as
Abel and Cain are brothers, or as Deutschland is "double a
desperate name" (l. 155), the name both of the ship and of a
country, a country which is itself double. Germany has given birth
both to a saint, Gertrude, lilylike in her purity, and to Luther, the
"beast of the waste wood" (ll. 157–58).

The theme of language in "The Wreck" moves toward the ambiguous vision of a God who is single but who can express himself in
language and in his creation only in the multiple. Though it takes
a "single eye" to "read the unshapeable shock night" (ll.
226–27)—that is, to see the unitary presence of God in the
storm—this insight must be expressed by the poet in multiple language. There is no masterword for the Word, only metaphors of it,
for all words are metaphors, displaced from their proper reference
by a primal bifurcation. When the tall nun "rears herself" (l. 150),
like "a lioness . . . breasting the babble" (l. 135), she is moving
back through the multiplicity of language (by way of the pun on
Babel) to the Word—Christ. But what the nun says must be interpreted ("the majesty! What did she mean?" [l. 193]), ultimately
moved back into the Babel or babble, the confusion of tongues introduced by Babel and confirmed by the gift of tongues at Pentecost.

In the same way the straightforward linear narrative of
Hopkins's poem is continuously displaced by all the echoes and
repetitions which turn the language of the poem back on itself in
lateral movements of meaning. These lateral relationships proliferate endlessly in multitudinous echoes. If Hopkins's basic poetic
strategy, as Geoffrey Hartman has noted, is a differentiation of language which attempts to say the Word by dividing the word, these
divisions are controlled by no central word which could be enun-
ciated in any language.[5]

Striking evidences revealing Hopkins's awareness of this tragic
eccentricity of the language of poetry appear in two crucial places

---

[5]See Geoffrey Hartman's "Hopkins Revisited," *Beyond Formalism* (New
Haven: Yale University Press, 1970), p. 239, where he speaks of "the tendency of
semantic distinctions to fall back into a phonemic ground of identity." "There is,
in other words," he continues, "a linguistic indifference against which language
contends, and contends successfully, by diacritical or differential means."

in the poem where the poet presents an ornate series of terms or metaphors for the same thing. In one case, significantly enough, the series names the act of writing, that act whereby God's finger inscribes his own name on those he has chosen, "his own bespoken" (l. 173). The stanza (22) presents a series of metaphors for the act of stamping something with a sign, making it a representation or metaphor of something else, man a metaphor of Christ. These are metaphors for metaphor:

> Five! the finding and sake
> And cipher of suffering Christ.
> Mark, the mark is of man's make
> And the word of it Sacrificed.
> But he scores it in scarlet himself on his own bespoken,
> Before-time-taken, dearest prizèd and priced—
> Stigma, signal, cinquefoil token
> For lettering of the lamb's fleece, ruddying of the rose-flake.

"Finding," "sake," "cipher," "mark," "word," "score," "stigma, signal, cinquefoil token," "lettering"—each is only one more word. The series is controlled by no unmoving word in any human language which would be outside the play of differentiations.

The other such list appears at the climax of the poem, the appearance of Christ to the nun at the moment of her death. It comes just after a passage in which the poet's syntactical control breaks down (the ellipses are Hopkins's): "But how shall I . . . make me room there: / Reach me a . . . fancy, come faster—" (ll. 217–18). Then follows a list of names for Christ. Significantly, this is the only place in the poem, and one of the few places in all Hopkins's English poetry, where the poet speaks with tongues himself and inserts a word not in his native language: "There then! the Master, / *Ipse,* the only one, Christ, King, Head" (ll. 220–21). The tragic limitation of poetic language lies in the fact that the Word itself cannot be said. Far from having a tendency to fall back into some undifferentiated ground of phonemic similarity (as Hartman affirms), a word by the very fact that it is just that pattern of vowels and consonants which it is, cannot be the Word. The words of human language, for Hopkins, seem to have been born of some primal division, a fall from the arch and original breath into the articulate. This fall has always already occurred as soon as there is any human speech. Words have therefore a tendency to proliferate endlessly their permutations by changes of vowel and consonant as if they were in search for the magic word that would be the Word. From this point of view it is surely significant that the original meaning lying behind most of the word lists in Hopkins's early diaries is one form or another of the gesture of dividing or marking. The sequence "flick, fleck, flake" is only one striking example of this. For Hopkins too the beginning is diacritical, an event of separation; and all word sequences may be followed back not to a primal unity but to a primal division or splitting. Even the intimate life of the Trinity, in which Hopkins was much interested, is characterized, for him, by the act whereby God divides himself from himself, goes outside himself, "as they say *ad extra*" (*Sermons*, p. 197).

The metaphor of language has a peculiar status in Hopkins's poem. It seems to be one model among others for the relation of nature to Christ or for the relation of the soul to Christ. A chain of such metaphors exists in Hopkins's poems and prose writings: music, echo, visible pattern or shape for nature's interrelations of "rhyme" in the connection of one item in nature to another and of each item to its model, Christ; cleave, sex, threshing, pitch (with a triple pun) for the action of grace on the soul. Along with the other items in the first sequence is the metaphor that says nature is interrelated in the way the words in a language are interrelated. This is one reason why Hopkins is so insistent that words should be onomatopoeic in origin. In the second sequence is included the metaphor that says the transformations of grace are like the changes from one word to another in a chain that goes from Jack to diamond. Christ is the Word on which all other words are modelled.

The difficulty raised by these terms in the two sequences is double. In the first place there is something odd about using as a model what in other cases has to be taken for granted as a transparent means of naming. Language about language has a different status from language about pomegranates being cloven, about threshing, or about sexual intercourse. Insofar as language emerges as the underthought of "The Wreck of the Deutschland," language in general and figure in particular are made problematical. They no longer can be taken for granted as adequate expressions of something extralinguistic. Second, this metaphor, like all the others, asks to be followed as far as it can be taken. When this happens in Hopkins's case, the whole structure of his thought and textual practice—theological, conceptual, or representational—is put in question by the fact that there is no master word, no word for the Word, only endless permutations. For Hopkins these permutations were not based on the emanation from a primal unity. The "origin" of language was that nonorigin which is a bifurcation, a bifurcation which, as soon as there is language at all, has always already taken place. It is this split, not unity, that is reached by a backward movement to the origin of language, as in the etymological speculations in Hopkins's early diaries, just as it is not "the Word" that is reached in "The Wreck of the Deutschland" or in "That Nature Is a Heraclitean Fire," but only another word, or a tautology: "diamond is diamond" in "That Nature Is a Heraclitean Fire," or the breakdown of language when Christ appears to the tall nun in "The Wreck of the Deutschland" or when the poet tries to describe the marking of man by Christ with the "stigma, signal, cinquefoil token."

There are indeed two texts in Hopkins, the overthought and the underthought. One text, the overthought, is a version (a particularly splendid version) of western metaphysics in its Catholic Christian form. In this text the Word governs all words, as it governs natural objects and selves. Like Father, like Son, and the sons are a way back to the Father. "No man cometh to the Father but by me" (John 14:6). On the other hand the underthought, if it is followed out, is a thought about language itself. It recognizes that there is no word for the Word, that all words are metaphors—that is, all are differentiated, differed, and deferred. Each leads to something of which it is the displacement in a movement without origin or end. Insofar as the play of language emerges as the basic model for the other two realms (nature and the effects of grace within the soul), it subverts both nature and supernature. The individual natural object and the individual self, by the fact of their individuality, are incapable of ever being more than a metaphor of Christ—that is, split off from Christ. They are incapable by whatever extravagant series of sideways transformations from ever becoming more than another metaphor. On the one hand, then, "No man cometh to the Father but by me," and on the other hand, "No one comes to the Father by imitating me, for I am the principle of distance and differentiation. I am a principle of splitting which is discovered to have always already occurred, however far back toward the primal unity one goes, even back within the bosom of the Trinity itself."

If the tragedy of language is its inability to say the Word, the mystery of the human situation, as Hopkins presents it, is parallel. The more a man affirms himself the more he affirms his eccentricity, his individuality, his failure to be Christ, or Christlike, an "AfterChrist," as Hopkins puts it (*Sermons*, p. 100). It is only by an unimaginable and, literally, unspeakable transformation, the transformation effected by grace, such as the nun's "conception" of Christ at the moment of her death in "The Wreck of the Deutschland," that the individual human being can be turned into Christ. The fact that this transformation is "past telling of tongue" in any words that say directly what they mean is indicated not only by the fact that the action of grace (both in this poem and throughout Hopkins) is always described in metaphor, but also by the fact that such a large number of incompatible metaphors are used, forging (ll. 73–74), sexual reproduction, speaking, eating and being eaten, threshing, rope-twisting, armed combat, change of pitch or angle ("she rears herself," l. 150), the last itself a triple pun.

To put this in terms of the linguistic metaphor: if Hopkins's poetic theory and practice are everywhere dominated by wordplay based on a recognition that the relation of rhyme is the echoing at a distance of entities which are similar but not identical, the change of man through grace into Christ is a transcendence of that distance and difference into identity, a change of play into reality in which the image becomes what it images: "It is as if a man said," writes Hopkins, "That is Christ playing at me and me playing at Christ, only that it is no play but truth; That is Christ *being me* and me being Christ" (*Sermons*, p. 154). "The Wreck of the Deutschland," like all the great poems of Hopkins's maturity, turns on a recognition of the ultimate failure of poetic language. Its failure is never to be able to express the inconceivable and unsayable mystery of how something which is as unique as a single word—that is, a created soul—may be transformed into the one Word, Christ, which is its model, without for all that ceasing to be a unique and individual self.[6]

[6]Kenneth Burke, in remarks about this paper after its presentation at the Ransom Symposium at Kenyon College in April of 1975, argued that I should add something about the multiple meaning of the word *wreck* in the title. The poem, he said, is about Hopkins's wreck. This was a powerful plea to relate the linguistic complexities, or tensions, back to their subjective counterparts. Much is at stake here. That the poem is a deeply personal document there can be no doubt. Its linguistic tensions are "lived," not mere "verbal play" in the negative sense. It has always been Kenneth Burke's great strength, as opposed to some present-day "structuralists" or "semiologists," never to neutralize literary language, never to make it into a tame conundrum or trivial crossword puzzle. For Burke literature is always incarnated in the flesh and blood and nerves of its writer or reader. In this he is true to his great exemplar, Sigmund Freud.

Nor can there be any doubt that in "The Wreck of the Deutschland" Hopkins is speaking of his own wreck in the sense of personal disaster, fragmentation, or blockage (with the pun, elsewhere used by Hopkins, on "reck" as "beware of," "take warning from"). Hopkins's experience of himself as a wreck was associated with his sense of impotence, with his inability ever to finish anything or to "breed one work that wakes" (*Poems*, p. 107), as in a moving late letter: "And there they lie and my old notebooks and beginnings of things, ever so many, which it seems to me might well have been done, ruins and wrecks" (*Letters*, 3:255).

The movement to resurrection and salvation in "The Wreck of the Deutschland" does not, I should agree, fully counterbalance the extraordinary expression of unresolved tension. Resolution, in the sense of the final untying of a blocking knot, always remains a future event in Hopkins's writing, and necessarily so, on the terms of his own theology. The danger in Burke's suggestion, however, is, as always, the possibility of a psychologizing reduction, the making of literature into no more than a reflection or representation of something psychic which precedes it and which could exist without it. I should prefer to see Hopkins's personal wreck as his inextricable involvement, "in flesh and in blood," in a chain or net of signs, figures, concepts, and narrative patterns. The exchanges, permutations, contradictions, latent aporias, untyings and typings of these elements he had the courage and the genius to "live through" in his writing and in his experience. Subjectivity, I am arguing, with all its intensities, is more a result than an origin. To set it first, to make an explanatory principle of it, is, as Nietzsche says, a metalepsis, putting late before early, effect before cause.

On a Shift in the Concept of Interpretation

Ralph Cohen

FOR MORE THAN a generation, interpretation of particular literary works has dominated American college classrooms and scholarly journals, and it has provided an important body of criticism. But interpretation as explication in the past few years has come under severe attack for its view of the literary work as well as its view of language, of history, and of the reader. How and why did this come about? This paper is an effort to explain the transformation of some critical tenets and their practice. It should be understood, to paraphrase John Crowe Ransom's words, as observations on the understanding of criticism.[1]

In 1949 René Wellek and Austin Warren published their *Theory of Literature*. This work was the first theoretical presentation of a position that had been known on the continent for more than twenty-five years. In it the authors presented a formalist theory that stressed the self-identity, the concrete particularity, of all literary works. This theory, as they acknowledged, arose out of a crisis in the humanities; in the jargon of our time it arose out of a failure of communication. The purpose of their theory of literary individuality, of a work as a self-contained whole, was to strike down narrow specialization in literary study. Their aim was to make the human values of literature accessible to a wider audience and, by doing so, to make readers capable of self-realization and fulfillment. They sought to do this by insisting on the autonomy of the individual work.

Why do we study Shakespeare? [wrote Wellek]. It is clear we are not primarily interested in what he has in common with all men, for we could then as well study any other man, nor are we interested in what he has in common with all Englishmen, all men of the Renaissance, all Elizabethans, all poets, all dramatists, or even all Elizabethan dramatists, because in that case we might just as well study Dekker or Heywood. We

---

[1] For a discussion of the shift in criticism that touches on some of the issues of this essay, see Gregory T. Polletta, "The Place and Performance of Criticism," *Issues in Contemporary Literary Criticism* (Boston: Atlantic Monthly Press, 1973), pp. 1–27, and the essays by Geoffrey Hartman and David Bleich cited below.

want rather to discover what is peculiarly Shakespeare's, what makes Shakespeare Shakespeare; and this is obviously a problem of individuality and value. Even in studying a period or movement or one specific national literature, the literary student will be interested in it as an individuality with characteristic features and qualities which set it off from other similar groupings.[2]

These critics saw interpretation as a problem of meaning, in which individual works, groups of works, or periods were to be grasped in terms of differentia. The critics sought to reestablish communication between reader and poem by demanding attention to formal features, to the poem as poem—not as biography, sociology, or history; and they found the human values of literature in the attention to the concrete particulars of the individual work. It was assumed that the discovery of these particulars made readers cognizant of the varieties of literary individuality—and in so doing made them capable of understanding their own greater potentialities for fulfillment.

The ends of the formalists can be seen from the questions that they posed as well as from the broad humanist aims to which they directed themselves. They saw interpretation as defining the pattern within a work, but they did not overlook information outside the work. They used internal and external data as guides to the pattern of the poem. For them dictionary meanings, description, and explanation constituted interpretation. "Description," wrote W. K. Wimsatt, "in the most direct sense moves inside the poem, accenting the parts and showing their relations. It may also, however, look outside the poem . . . *Internal* and *external* are complementary. The external includes all the kinds of history in which the poem has its setting. A specially important kind of history, for example, is the literary tradition itself." According to Wimsatt, through description we arrive at a pattern "of the main formally controlling purpose in the well-written poem," and it is the implicit meaning of the whole that controls the meaning of the parts. Explanation of the external and description of the internal: these he sums up in "some such generic term as *elucidation* or *interpretation*."[3]

The insistence on the formally controlling purpose, the literary individuality of a work, led these critics, however, to exclude from literature Saint Augustine's *Confessions*, Pope's letters, and all

[2] *Theory of Literature*, 2d ed. (New York: Harcourt, Brace, 1956), p. 6.
[3] "What to Say about a Poem," *Hateful Contraries: Studies in Literature and Criticism* (Lexington: University of Kentucky Press, 1965), pp. 224, 226, 230.

works which were not marked by literariness—that is, by being fictive sign structures. This made it possible for them to see literature as a thoroughly consistent body of works, in which common ends provided a basis for systematic classifications and common values a basis for distinguishing literary from nonliterary endeavors. But the consequence of this procedure was not to increase literature's role in shaping the individual's self-realization in society; instead it proved a means for avoiding or neglecting such roles. The subtlety of literary analysis of individual poems was surely increased, but the insistence on the purely literary function of the analysis served to heighten rather than control the crisis it was meant to solve.

It did this by turning the reading of literature into an examination of objects rather than into a dynamic relationship between reader and work. When a distinguished critic, Reuben Brower, wrote an essay in 1959 on how he taught literature at Harvard, he declared that teachers of literature are especially concerned "with teaching ways of discovering and experiencing values expressed through literary objects. The most precious thing they can give their students is some increase of power, some help however humble in getting into Shakespeare or Dr. Johnson or Joyce." Now this view of the literary work as an object, as a kind of isolated phenomenon with a structure that controlled rather than cooperated with the reader, led to a series of specific questions that these critics asked about the work. The *help* that was given the reader was of the following kind:

"What is it *like* . . . to read this poem?" "With what feeling are we left at its close?" "What sort of person is speaking?" "What is he *like* and where does he reveal himself most clearly?" "In what line or phrase?" We may then ask if there is a key phrase or word in the poem, and we can begin to introduce the notion of the poem as a structure, as an ordered experience built up through various kinds of meaning controlled in turn by various uses of language.[4]

These questions reveal to the reader how the structure of the poem controls his response; they provide a coherent basis for the internal relations of the poem, for its specific language uses. These were important to Brower because they compelled the reader to recognize the autonomous existence of the art object. To study the

[4]"Reading in Slow Motion," *In Defense of Reading: A Reader's Approach to Literary Criticism*, ed. Reuben A. Brower and Richard Poirier (New York: Dutton, 1963), pp. 20, 12.

poem is not to study ideas, historical backgrounds, biographical references, but rather the work's self-contained, reflexive, nonreferential values. Paradoxically the social aim of literature was the underlying rationale for engaging in such study. Whatever the purely literary values were, their justification was in their applicability to, and function in, society. And these literary practices have called into question the achievement of the social aims.

It was indeed a paradox that the concept of individuality should be advanced as a basis for communal understanding. The dilemma might be put this way: only as we recognize the uniqueness of each work as literature will we be able to assess its contribution to the shared responses of the human community. Even the very act of identification or assessment posits a social relationship based on similarity as well as difference. The reader's relation to a work begins with the hypothesis that it is or is not literature. The notion of what "literature" is will specify a relation to the human community. If one accepts prison narratives or letters, journals, sermons, indeed, any writing as a form of literature, one is not involved in distinguishing what is from what is not literature. To ask whether a textbook or newspaper article is literature is to make apparent the arbitrariness of the answer. It is literature if the definition includes it; it is not if the definition excludes it. But on what foundation does the definition rest?

The definition of literature is necessarily dependent on the critic's view of language in society, of the kind of distinctions he makes between verbal and nonverbal behavior, and of the principle of classification he accepts. "Literariness," to be viable, necessarily depends on knowing what is nonliterariness.[5] The formalists' concern with the individual, their refinement of special literary skills, their reference to objective structures (works) that elicited responses—all of these took for granted the knowledge of the individual who reads, the meanings he creates, the responses he makes. And we can understand the need for their questions about individual works when students have lost touch with the artistic possibilities of such works: William Wimsatt's address "What to Say about a Poem" was, after all, presented to teachers. As teachers we recognize how important it was to free poems from the fact-gathering, positivistic procedures that then engulfed them.

[5] For a discussion of this subject, see John M. Ellis, "The Definition of Literature," *The Theory of Literary Criticism: A Logical Analysis* (Berkeley: University of California Press, 1974), pp. 24–53, and the symposium "What Is Literature?" *New Literary History*, 5 (Autumn 1973).

What Wimsatt and his colleagues of similar persuasion were resisting was the sociological and historical study of literature. What, then, is calling explication as interpretation into question?

This method is being called into question. Geoffrey Hartman, for example, believes that "explication-centered criticism is indeed puerile"; "we forget its merely preparatory function." The end of criticism ought to be a study of poetic consciousness; it ought to raise interpretation "to its former state of confronting art with experience as searchingly as if art were scripture."[6] Hartman seeks to redefine interpretation by relating it to the poet's understanding of experience, in which he includes the poet's understanding of earlier poets. And the relating is, of course, done by an interpreter so that the self-consciousness of the latter becomes a necessity for criticism. Harold Bloom also rejects the earlier view of interpretation as "practical criticism" by arguing that no poem is an autonomous object. "I propose, not another new poetics, but a wholly different practical criticism. Let us give up the failed enterprise of seeking to 'understand' any single poem as an entity in itself. Let us pursue instead the quest of learning to read any poem as its poet's deliberate misinterpretation, *as a poet*, of a precursor poem or of poetry in general."[7]

In these two Yale-trained critics, and in the writings of a third, Stanley Fish, we find efforts to redefine interpretation, not to overthrow it. These redefinitions include the expansion of interpretation in terms of the poet's consciousness, the necessity of the self-awareness of the critic, the consideration of the "influence" of other poems upon the poet, and, for Fish, the reconsideration of meaning in terms of the educated reader. It is important to recognize that while "correcting" earlier "interpretative" criticism, these critics present new difficulties. They raise objections to those aspects of interpretation that minimize the network of relationships between works, of meaning to language, of the reader's response to the work. But Geoffrey Hartman's view of the poet's consciousness seems to depend on the critic's consciousness rather than on any more stable guide. And Harold Bloom's view that poems are known by misinterpretation creates a logical

---

[6]"Beyond Formalism," *Beyond Formalism: Literary Essays, 1958–1970* (New Haven: Yale University Press, 1970), pp. 54, 57. For a statement about the interpreter, see Hartman's "The Interpreter: A Self-Analysis," *The Fate of Reading and Other Essays* (Chicago: University of Chicago Press, 1975), pp. 3–19.

[7]*The Anxiety of Influence: A Theory of Poetry* (New York: Oxford University Press, 1973), p. 43.

and historical puzzle since misinterpretation presupposes a correct interpretation that has no existence. Consider, for example, the criticism of Stanley Fish:

What I am suggesting is that there is no direct relationship between the meaning of a sentence (paragraph, novel, poem) and what its words mean. Or, to put the matter less provocatively, the information an utterance gives, its message, is a constituent of, but certainly not to be identified with, its meaning. It is the experience of an utterance—*all* of it and not anything that could be said about it, including anything I could say—that *is* its meaning.[8]

This statement does not deny the need for Wimsatt's explanation—the need to look up the meanings of words or names—but it does deny that such information can be identified with the "meaning of a poem." The message is a "constituent of meaning," but the "experience of an utterance" includes more than the message. It is the theory of meaning divorced from the historical or conventional expectations of the reader that is being questioned, and the objection is lodged against the *assumed* objectivity or neutrality of the reader. Reading is an activity and the reader is an "actively mediating presence." Stanley Fish talks about "meaning as event"; that is, meaning is a result of a reader experiencing a poem or a prose work.[9]

Now this sounds very much like a formalist position developed by René Wellek, who wrote: "What the formalist wants to maintain is that the poem is not only a cause, or a potential cause, of the reader's 'poetic experience' but a specific, highly organized control of the reader's experience, so that the experience is most fittingly described as an experience of the poem."[10] Although the two statements refer to experience, they do not share a common view of it. For Wellek, the "experience" is a reader's response to carefully organized words, lines, and sentences. These control his response. For Stanley Fish "the experience of an utterance" is a reader's response to the expectations of words, lines, and sentences. Wellek's reader's response leads to the question "What does this mean?"; but Fish's asks: "What does this do?"

Fish discusses the following passage from *Paradise Lost* after Satan addresses the fallen angels lying on the lake of Hell.

[8]"Literature in the Reader: Affective Stylistics," *Self-Consuming Artifacts: The Experiences of Seventeenth-Century Literature* (Berkeley: University of California Press, 1972), p. 393.
[9]Ibid., p. 384.
[10]*Theory of Literature*, p. 261.

> They heard, and were abasht, and up they sprung
> Upon the wing; as when men wont to watch
> On duty, sleeping found by whom they dread,
> Rouse and bestir themselves ere well awake.
> Nor did they not perceive the evil plight
> In which they were, or the fierce pains not feel;
> Yet to thir General's voice they soon obey'd
> Innumerable.
>
> [I, 331–38]

Fish selects the line "Nor did they not perceive the evil plight" and writes his experience of it:

The first word of this line from *Paradise Lost* (I, 335) generates a rather precise (if abstract) expectation of what will follow: a negative assertion which will require for its completion a subject and a verb. There are then two "dummy" slots in the reader's mind waiting to be filled. This expectation is strengthened (if only because it is not challenged) by the auxiliary "did" and the pronoun "they." Presumably, the verb is not far behind. But in its place the reader is presented with a second negative, one that can not be accommodated within his projection of the utterance's form. His progress through the line is halted and he is forced to come to terms with the intrusive (because unexpected) "not." In effect what the reader *does*, or is forced to do, at this point, is ask a question—did they or didn't they?—and in search of an answer he either rereads, in which case he simply repeats the sequence of mental operations, or goes forward, in which case he finds the anticipated verb, but in either case the syntactical uncertainty remains unresolved. . . .

Underlying [this analysis] is a method, rather simple in concept, but complex (or at least complicated) in execution. The concept is simply the rigorous and distinterested asking of the question, what does this word, phrase, sentence, paragraph, chapter, novel, play, poem, *do?*; and the execution involves *an analysis of the developing responses of the reader in relation to the words as they succeed one another in time.*[11]

Fish's "experiencing" of this line from *Paradise Lost* demonstrates what he means by experiencing the utterance and how he answers the question, "What does this word, phrase . . . do?" He begins with a line, a part of a sentence with a compound verb—"perceive" and "feel." The ambiguous response that is elicited is a result of not completing the sentence: "What is a problem if the line is considered as an object, a thing-in-itself, becomes a *fact* when it is regarded as an occurrence."[12] The rejection of Wimsatt's treatment of the poem as object becomes in this

[11] *Self-Consuming Artifacts*, pp. 386–88.
[12] Ibid., p. 387.

procedure a treatment of the word or line as object, as thing-in-it-self; words or lines are entities that succeed one another in time. Thus the emendation of a view of language creates new difficulties about the nature of reading. And this appears in Fish's analysis of the passage.

The problem for Fish is to provide a new view of a reader whose subjectivity attends to Milton's use of diction and syntax without denying that he is a twentieth-century reader. Stanley Fish realizes that his reader responds in terms of his expectations. "I would rather," he writes, "have an acknowledged and controlled sub-jectivity than an objectivity which is finally an illusion." He calls, therefore, for a critic who "has the responsibility of becoming not one but a number of informed readers, each of whom will be identified by a matrix of political, cultural and literary de-terminants. The informed reader of Milton will not be the in-formed reader of Whitman."[13] But the difficulty with such injunc-tions is how a reader becomes informed, for readers like Wimsatt and Brower are informed readers, and they wish to inform other readers. Indeed it is apparent that Fish is offering a variant of Brower's "Reading in Slow Motion."[14]

For Brower and for Wimsatt the student is the reader who is to be taught language discrimination and certain literary values im-plicit in literary works. But such aims presuppose that the theory of language used offers a proper basis for discriminations, that the works chosen will provide proper values to be discriminated, and that the readers will constitute a group who share cultural values. Fish's emendation is to erect language into a kind of absolute so that the intelligent reader will respond to it in terms of proper ex-pectations. It is not the concept of the reader that is altered, only the language used to describe him. Thus for Fish responses to lan-guage become a "theory" of affects.

Fish argues for the continuity of ordinary and poetic language. He seeks to avoid the assumed disparity between poetic and or-dinary language. And he does so in order to establish a comple-mentarity between literary and nonliterary language, a relation

[13] This and the question immediately preceding are from Fish, p. 407. The em-phasis on the subjectivity of the reader takes several forms in recent criticism. See, for example, David Bleich, "The Subjective Character of Critical Interpretation," *College English*, 36 (1975), 739–55.

[14] Fish even uses Brower's terms: "Essentially what the method does is *slow down* the reading experience so that 'events' one does not notice in normal time, but which do occur, are brought before our analytical attentions" (Fish, p. 389).

that makes literature subject to the same rhetorical and evaluative procedures as those governing ordinary language. He thus seeks to give to the study of literature a range of value that makes it applicable to all uses of language in society. And he seeks, too, in his interpretation of the reader or speaker, to remove the so-called objectivity of the literary responder.

Curiously enough [writes Claudio Guillén], it was a physicist, Niels Bohr, who stressed the truism that "we are both actors and spectators in the great drama of existence." . . . "Natural science," Werner Heisenberg writes, "does not simply explain and describe nature; it is a part of the interplay between nature and ourselves; it describes nature as exposed to our method of questioning. . . ." Similarly, the contemporary arts are no longer devoted to a description of nature based on a sharp separation between the world and the I.[15]

The alteration, even the supersession, of the formalist premises occurs in at least three ways. With regard to language, the analyses of meaning in Wimsatt's or Brower's sense are found to be inadequate because such analyses no longer confirm how words mean. With regard to the reader's relation to a work, the subjective (or affective or Freudian) responses become primary because the reader is the valued being in the relationship. Finally, with regard to contemporary affairs or history, the premises cease to be appropriate to literary activities because they lack the values such activities are supposed to have. The loss of the reader's interest in the study of literature can be seen as a consequence of the shift in values about the nature of language and of learning.

This is apparent in the relation of interpretation to a Freudian and Marxist theory of meaning in the work of Fredric Jameson. He writes that "the process of criticism is not so much an interpretation of content as it is a revealing of it, a laying bare, a restoration of the original message, the original experience, beneath the distortions of the censor: and this revelation takes the form of an explanation why the content was so distorted; it is inseparable from a description of the mechanism of censorship itself." For him the language of a literary work implies a censored message in addition to the stated content, and this message in our time is a social one. The value in this criticism, as Jameson sees it, lies in its understanding of how art conceals social manipulation. Interpretation

<hr>

[15]Claudio Guillén, "On the Concept and Metaphor of Perspective," *Literature as System: Essays toward the Theory of Literary History* (Princeton: Princeton University Press, 1971). p. 371.

becomes, therefore, not a guide to the individuality of the writer, but to the society of which he is a part. The work of art

obeys a double impulse: on the one hand, it preserves the subject's fitful contact with genuine life. . . . And on the other, its mechanisms function as a censorship whose task is to forestall any conscious realization on the part of the subject of his own impoverishment; and to prevent him from drawing any practical conclusions as to the causes for that impoverishment and mutilation, and as to their origin in the social system itself.[16]

The formalists attended to the reader's involvement in the work. But the involvement was seen as "objective"; they attended to the nature of the work in terms of norms, agreeing that many interpretations were possible, but they denied that the work was a *censored* language structure; they attended to meaning, but not meaning as reader's response. Jameson's view that the message of every poem is a censored language structure presupposes that all censorship is social and that poetic language has a special quality. It is a questionable position to take, though there is no need to deny that some kinds of language do conceal censored situations. Thus his revision of interpretation points to a problematic area that earlier critics assumed was without difficulties.

The formalist views arose to answer the need for individuality of the work; this constituted the basis for their values and their moral aims. What has come to be questioned is precisely this individuality. I have suggested that the objections to the formalist position arose from literary inadequacies, but I should add that the classroom, because it is the institution that tests literary claims, becomes another guide to the ineffectiveness of a literary hypothesis. If the purpose of asking questions about meaning is to give the student an opportunity for making discriminations in language, and if such questions no longer confirm how words mean, they cease to be appropriate to the activities of those to whom they are directed. The loss of the reader's interest in the study of literature can be partially seen as a consequence of inadequate questions. The readers were constantly exposed to an unsound rhetoric, a language that concealed meanings, that had first to be mastered in order to be understood. The need to provide different questions

---

[16]"Metacommentary," *PMLA*, 86 (1971), 16–17. The non-Freudian view that language is by its very nature only partially *expressed* and partially suspended can be found in the work of philosophers and critics, e.g., Ludwig Wittgenstein, *Tractatus Logico-Philosophicus*, trans. D. F. Pears and B. F. McGuinnis (1922; rpt. London: Routledge and Kegan Paul, 1971), pp. 35–37, and Serge Doubrovsky, *The New Criticism in France* (Chicago: University of Chicago Press, 1973), p. 241.

arose, then, from the reader's awareness of how language was used in society in contrast to how it was being taught in the classroom.

The alternative now being posited is that readers in relation to works are conspirators or collaborators who decode the conscious form, and the idea of the individual work as an object is being supplanted by the work as event. This essay can be understood as an inquiry into two types of interpretative relationship: that of the critic who seeks to reveal the complicated but overt form of a poem and the relationship which is replacing this—that of the critic who reveals this consciousness of, or his consciousness of his responses to, the poem. In the first procedure the critic seeks to discover the identity and individuality of a given poetic form; in the second the critic seeks to move from a given poetic form to another underlying form. If the first had self-realization as its social aim, the second substitutes awareness of self (for self-realization) and awareness of institutional manipulation.

The shift in interpretation has redeveloped a critical trust in historical and theoretical premises: that is, the setting up of hypotheses of historical or psychological continuity which provide a basis for coherent literary study—while rejecting the overt model of the formalists. One is Frye's archetypes in which the series of historical-literary changes (myth, romance, high mimetic, low mimetic, ironic) and the very model of literature is identified with persisting archetypal narratives. Interpretation is necessarily ancillary to the analysis of enduring narrative since any individual example is a reworking of a myth. And when Harold Bloom abandoned close analysis for a theory of poetic influence, he recognized that he was giving priority to the historical responsiveness of one poet to another, to the relation of a poem to its predecessor: a theory that made individual interpretation an inevitable mistake.

Bloom's question about the deliberate altering of a past poem (or concept of poetry) draws attention to the reassertion of historical inquiry, one which focuses upon the present's changing of the past. In this respect the shift in questions that I have been tracing is a shift from practical analysis to theoretical inquiry, from the study of relations within a work to the study of relations among works, from history as secondary to history as primary.

The study of interpretation as explication has been altered in terms of the nature of the concrete particularity of a work, in terms of the theory of meaning, in terms of the historical interrelation of works, and in terms of the response of the reader. Nevertheless it must be acknowledged that the social aims of criticism continue, that the need to understand the individual work persists, that the need to explain words, rhyme schemes, and meters persists. Thus, if we conceive of criticism as dealing with the varied aspects of a problem, it becomes possible to identify those aspects that are called into question and those that persist. The redirecting of the inquiry leads to questions that had been minimized, overlooked, or misunderstood. But the change inevitably introduces theoretical inquiries since the specific examples cannot, in themselves, be the grounds for a rejection of a procedure.

In this respect the positing of alternatives to formalism is part of a larger movement in western criticism than the American experience indicates. For Georges Poulet, for example, the under-standing of an individual work is dependent on the writer's total work; a writer's meaning, his private dictionary, is available only if one can provide hypotheses by which his identity can be realized in quite different works. In such a theory the critic rejects the prin-ciple of interpretative wholeness within the single work and considers the single poem, novel, or essay as mere parts of a more comprehensive analysis of a writer's mode of thought and feeling. The reader is seen as necessarily involved in the creation of the work; the problem is the nature of the reader's self. It is important to grasp the shift in the problem because this inquiry has to be answered before the work can be interpreted. Poulet suggests that the reader brings the work into his own consciousness, that the process of reading requires the critic to reconstruct the artist's cate-gories of thought, of space and time.[17]

If Poulet's phenomenological view has the reader as reconstruc-tionist of the artist's categories, the aesthetics of response has the scholar as reconstructionist of critical interpretations. The aesthetics of response arose, as Hans Robert Jauss makes clear, as an attempt to move beyond the limits of formalism and Marxism. It provides a stock-taking of intelligent responses to a work throughout its history. The theory assumes that at different times different critical questions about the literary work are inevitable and that, therefore, the primary concern of the critic is to chart the different answers or interpretations.

For the aesthetics-of-response critics the important question is *not*, what are the kinds of meaning controlled by language, *not*

[17] See *Studies in Human Time* (Baltimore: Johns Hopkins University Press, 1956), *The Interior Distance* (Baltimore: Johns Hopkins University Press, 1959), and "Phenomenology of Reading," *NLH*, 1 (1969), 53–68.

what does this word or phrase do, *but* "why do critics at different times ask different interpretative questions?" These response critics begin with three distinctions: text, interpretation, and literary work. The text is the author's words on the page; interpretation is a construction by a single reader of statements giving coherence to attitudes in the text; and the literary work is a sum of interpretations. For this criticism, interpretation is necessary, but it has become subsidiary to a metainterpretative theory—one that relates all given interpretations as a dialogue. "The historicity of literature," writes H. R. Jauss, "presupposes a relationship of work, audience and new work which takes the form of a dialogue as well as a process, and which can be understood in the relationship of message and receiver . . . question and answer, problem and solution."[18]

For Jauss the *historical* situation of the reader is responsible for the kind of questions that he asks and the kind of answers he gives. He thus assumes that each interpretation provides a way of conceiving of a text and each is replaced by a subsequent interpretation. In this argument, interpretation becomes subordinate to the kinds of questions that a critic poses, for such questions are appropriate only to particular moments in history.

Having extended my discussion to include European critics, I wish now to suggest some social and political reasons for the shift. The dissolving of the work as a concrete particular is part of a more general attack on the positivism (or atomizing) of human relationships. The arguments against the particularity of the work rest on the intertwining of reader and work in which the latter requires the former for its "completion." But not completion in the sense of a whole: every response to a work is based on a reader's perspective—and this changes in time. This argument may, perhaps, be seen as leading to the conclusion that a work is not one concrete particular but many. This would, however, be a mistake. A literary work is not a concrete particular because the language and the form are dependent for their definition upon other works of the same writer or / and prior forms and conventions.

This hypothesis is thus connected with the theory of how a work means. The work is taken for granted as a historical entity, and it is historical and personal in its use of language. The writer is seen as operating within a society in which, at times, he conceals as well as

---

[18]"Literary History as a Challenge to Literary Theory," *New Directions in Literary History*, ed. Ralph Cohen (Baltimore: Johns Hopkins University Press, 1974), p. 12.

reveals his message. And as an individual his language has, inevitably, private aspects. This hypothesis has its sources in the restrictions and oppressions of democratic and nondemocratic societies, and, on a personal level, it insists on the linguistic complexity of the writer and reader. Implicit in this view is a rejection of ideal levels of language for a historical view that language is inevitably acculturated so that any particular use of it inevitably contains more implication than the writer and the reader are aware of. The need to reach both levels of language requires the critic to intuit a writer's grammar or to grasp his work as a whole or to provide a special mode of reading.

The revised approach to meaning can take several forms, but all of them presuppose that the poem is a historical and cultural work. As such these critics are concerned with the readers' changes of interpretation. The awareness of such changes seems to be connected with a knowledge of political manipulation, political oppression and suppression. The revised literary interpretation develops a view that the responses of men must be revealed and understood, that differences in responses must be accepted as given. Thus the aesthetics of response or "affective stylists" or the justification, in psychological terms, of a multiplicity of responses provides a basis for acceptance of individual and cultural differences.

I have sought to explain why explicative interpretation has begun to be insufficient for contemporary critics. It now remains for me to illustrate how this applies to the interpretation of a poem. How different, how new, would such an interpretation be? The phenomenologically oriented studies of Poulet, Geoffrey Hartman, and J. Hillis Miller represent one type of this new mode of interpretation. The recent work of Harold Bloom in *A Map of Misreading* represents another, as do the works of Norman Holland and Wolfgang Iser. I wish to offer still another variant—interpretation in terms of the functions of literary conventions—to suggest the range of these alternatives to formalism.

I select as my example Blake's "London" because it has been carefully studied.[19]

---

[19]"Genesis: A Fallacy Revisited," *The Disciplines of Criticism: Essays in Literary Theory, Interpretation, and History,* ed. Peter Demetz, Thomas Greene, and Lowry Nelson, Jr. (New Haven: Yale University Press, 1968), p. 217. Cleanth Brooks and Robert Penn Warren in *Understanding Poetry,* rev. ed. (New York: Holt, 1953) ask the following questions about the poem: "1. What is the meaning of *chartered* in lines 1 and 2? What does the poet gain by repeating *mark* in lines 3

I wander thro' each charter'd street
Near where the charter'd Thames does flow,
And mark in every face I meet
Marks of weakness, marks of woe.

In every cry of every Man,
In every Infant's cry of fear,
In every voice, in every ban,
The mind-forg'd manacles I hear.

How the Chimney-sweeper's cry
Every black'ning Church appalls;
And the hapless Soldier's sigh
Runs in blood down Palace walls.

But most thro' midnight streets I hear
How the youthful Harlot's curse
Blasts the new-born Infant's tear,
And blights with plagues the Marriage hearse.

Mr. Wimsatt points out the need to look up words like "charter'd" and to recognize the verse form as that of eighteenth-century evangelical hymns. This poem of the dark city, he writes, "is about human 'weakness' and 'woe' as they may be observed in certain (uncertain) visual and auditory betrayals ('marks' and 'cries') and in certain (uncertain) imputed human causes (charters, bans, mind-forged manacles)." This pattern is developed by repetitions, ambiguities (of cries and marks), by constants of "black" and "appall," developed even "beyond verbalism into the bold, surrealistically asserted vision of the *sigh* which attaches itself as blood to palace walls."[20]

Surely one would want to agree with Wimsatt in his explanatory level (chartered, marks)—such repetitions do exist; so, too, with

---

and 4? Does it have the effect of childish repetition? Or what? 2. In the eighteenth century, children were employed as chimney-sweepers. Does this help account for the fact that the chimney-sweeper's cry appalls the church? 3. The speaker says that he hears the 'mind-forged manacles' in every cry. In what sense do the various cries mentioned come under this description? Does the youthful harlot's voice serve as a climax to these cries? How?" (pp. 427–28). For interpretations of this poem that seek to depart from the formalist premises, see Harold Bloom, *The Visionary Company: A Reading of English Romantic Poetry* (New York: Doubleday, 1961), pp. 42–43, and E. D. Hirsch, *Innocence and Experience: An Introduction to Blake* (New Haven: Yale University Press, 1968), pp. 263–65. In his essay of 1968 William Wimsatt reaffirms his earlier statements about "London" by attacking Hirsch's "intentionalist" reading.

[20] *Hateful Contraries*, p. 237.

the effect of "a bitter chanting, a dark repetition of indictments."
So, too, his historical—in the sense of the eighteenth-century back-
ground—explanation of London "cries" is as perceptive and accurate as is the reference to the verse form.

But the postformalist or conceptualist position I am urging, in
considering the simple hymnlike stanzas, will want to ask, "How in
adapting eighteenth-century conventions does Blake imply a rejection of previous functions?" And how does the verse form function
for him?

> In every cry of every Man,
> In every Infant's cry of fear,
> In every voice, in every ban,
> The mind-forg'd manacles I hear.

The balanced line and the parallelism are typical procedures of the
couplet, and they are used in eighteenth-century poetry to indicate
contrasts that are harmoniously confused, instances of variety that
are to be subsumed under a common nature, alternatives that complement one another. What Blake is doing is taking a metrical form
marked by excessive poetic order—repetition, balance, control—and using it as a chant in which control is defined by chaining
or "manacling." The simplicity and songlike order of the stanza is
in direct contrast to the hysteria of the diction.

The *adaptation* of conventions, not their identification, is the
pertinent emphasis in this criticism, and what Blake seems to be
implying is that the inherited convention serves as terrorizing control despite its apparent innocuousness.

Here it is necessary to point out that the internal-external relation—the notice of external marks of internal suffering—identified
by Wimsatt needs to be converted into a question. How does Blake
use language so that it possesses the experience that he wishes to
convey? This is a question about Blake's poetic identity in language, and its answer requires some hypotheses about his work as a
whole, especially about his work up to and including *Songs of
Experience*. Consider the relation of "mark" to "marks of
woe"—the movement of verb to noun, of action (noticing) to object (marks). Blake implies a reflexive relation between doing and
being insofar as "seeing," "hearing," and "observing" are mere
perceptual acts; it is an implied commentary on the eighteenth-
century convention of the spectator, the distanced observer, the
uninvolved wanderer. Blake's language in this respect indicates
that the speaker sees and hears the cries that are the cries of pain or

consequences of corruption, but there remains an unbridged distance, a distance that needs to be bridged, between the observer and the corrupters and the victims of corruption—the implication being that there is a reflexive relation between the speaker and both victor and victim.

In referring to the social implications of the uninvolved spectator, I am drawing attention to the literary and cultural functions of a rhetorical feature, not merely identifying it. So, too, I wish to discuss the idea of a reader of eighteenth-century poetry, of Blake's poetry; without raising the question of how learned he is, this much should be agreed upon. No reader of Thomas Gray's "Elegy" had a knowledge of "London," but it is possible for a reader of "London" to have knowledge of the "Elegy."

Let me introduce the expectations of a reader educated in the reading of poetry before Blake. Here is a stanza from Gray's "Elegy."

> Now fades the glimmering landscape on the sight,
>   And all the air a solemn stillness holds,
> Save where the beetle wheels his droning flight,
>   And drowsy tinklings lull the distant folds.

The "glimmering landscape," "solemn stillness," "droning flight," "drowsy tinklings," "distant folds"—here we have a convention in which a representative adjective has as its aim the capture of a typical moment in time. Each adjective-noun cluster tends to support or complement every other to form a harmony at sunset. Blake's handling of this convention illuminates both his view of the past and his way of thinking. He also uses adjective-noun combinations—"every cry," "every Man"—but these refer to all, not to representative instances. And he introduces a whole series of nonadjectives that function as adjectives in combination: the noun as possessive—"Infant's cry," "Soldier's sigh"; the noun-verb—"mind-forg'd; the noun-noun—"Palace walls," "midnight streets," "Marriage hearse"; the verb-noun—"charter'd streets." We can note in this grammatical procedure the manner in which the whole—the person (infant), place (palace), institution (church)—is made to modify a part. The cry represents the infant; the sigh, the soldier; the curse, the harlot. In the "charter'd streets" the streets become identified with privilege, and in the "midnight streets" streets refers to recurrent time. Blake's adjective-noun constructions serve to implicate actions and people and institutions—so that the infant, soldier, chimney sweep, and harlot

reflect the "mind-forg'd manacles." The external cries of inner
feeling touch only the externals of church or palace. What Blake is
doing to the convention is indicating the relation between parts
and wholes in which the procedure of valued, perceptual normality
and typicality has been inverted and become indicative of the inner
despair and institutional disregard.

Thus interpretation of "London" becomes a study of the historical analysis of values through conventions, and although this is
only one incomplete example, it sees the poem as a songlike religious ritual, with an inherited order, terrifying in its uniformity,
converting life to death. And it does this by an implied historical
revision of inherited practices. Interpretation ceases to be an interpretation of the individual poem and becomes an analysis of the
changes in the function of its conventions. Interpretation is thus
dependent upon prior poems and poetic styles, explaining their
functions with regard to parts and the whole.

My analysis can, in one sense, be seen as developing from the
formalist interest in language analysis, in relation of parts to
wholes, in the recognition of the role of tradition. But in another
sense the premises of this analysis call the grounds of formalism
into question. The focus of the analysis is not the poem but the
changing conventions and their functions; thus the idea of the
poem as an autonomous object is rejected since the poem is both
defined and analyzed with reference to prior uses of conventions.
The formal language analysis is not supported by the part-whole
procedure but by a historical hypothesis about the cultural nature
of conventions. And the reader moves to the foreground of the
analysis by relating conventions to social action, denying the
nonreferentiality of the work as well as the formalist implication of
self-realization. Finally the analysis draws attention to the poem's
function as an implied critical statement rejecting the earlier uses
of a convention because of its support of insupportable institutions.

Explicative interpretation was "sufficient" for the premises of
formalist criticism because these were directly related to the individuality of the work as object. It is not, and cannot be, sufficient
for a criticism governed by the premises that language is acculturated and that the literary work does not have an objective life
aside from interpreters, "objective life" now referring to the
phenomena of readers as social beings.

Explicative interpretation is insufficient to account for the new
view of the literary work as event, for the historicity of literary language and form, for the nature of the reader's response. These lead

to a redefinition of interpretation as a study of the poet's consciousness or the reader's response. They also lead to a study of the interpretation of forms or conventions which are prior to interpretation. For this criticism a different sufficiency of interpretation is
necessary even though it can include some of the earlier premises
and revise others.

But neither this emended criticism nor any other criticism has
proved to be more than sufficient unto the day. The speculative
leaps in characterizing the reader and in the analyses of history and
of forms are already apparent. Criticism, and, within it, any kind of
interpretation, is based on a social vision, the state of knowledge
governing the self, the literary structures, the available texts. As
these change so do the premises of interpretation.

On Literary Form

Kenneth Burke

IN REGARD TO memories in connection with this particular occasion I would like to say that, along with my gratitude for the many kindnesses John Crowe Ransom granted me in his role as the generous and exceptionally humane editor of the *Kenyon Review*, I most warmly recall an almost songful summer session when he and Richard Blackmur and I shared an idyllic house and garden on the edge of the campus in Bloomington. Progress has caught up to it now: it's just a parking lot; they ripped the whole place out. Ransom's subtle combination of friendliness and distance was a remarkable experience in itself for one to encounter. He spontaneously made one want to do one's best, and one felt quite good whenever Ransom seemed inclined to go along with something one cared about. If a great sense of gratitude to him, and admiration for him, are the tests, then surely I qualify to be among those invited to participate in this occasion.

I want to make a few comments in relation to the previous papers and then pull things together. There's one point on this whole issue about the specialization of literature and so on—that problem kept turning up. I don't see any problem there. I had to meet a condition of this kind, and I've gone on with it for many years and worked it out this way. That is, here's what you would say about a work if you didn't even know who wrote it. If you take the work just as it is, it's completely anonymous, and you have certain things to say about it on that basis. For instance you consider it along the lines of Aristotle: it has a beginning, a middle, and an end. Where does it start? Where does it go through and where does it end? It's right there. Someone else might want to disagree with the way you set it up, but at least you've got the issue right there to see how you worked it out. Every work has a set of equations in it. These equations in philosophy are made specific. The only case at the moment that I recall that specific equation in poetry, however, is where William Carlos Williams said that a city is a person. He's worked out that notion. There's something of that sort in what some of the philosophers say. Berkeley says, "*Esse est percipere*"—to be is to be perceived. A whole line follows from

that. And Spinoza says, *"Dio es natura"*; he's equated God and nature: God equals nature, and a whole set of developments follows
from that. I think that what you have in a work is implicitly in it; if
you don't say it explicitly you have a set of equations. This is the
only way you can write: something equals cowardice, something
equals heroism, something equals the desirable, something equals
the undesirable, and so on. Now *that* you can deal with just the
way the work is, right in front of your eyes.

There are many elements in the individual work, but if you knew
more about the author's nomenclature—say you knew other poems
of his—lots of the terms that are not fully developed there you
could fill out by talking about some of his other poems, by seeing
how those same terms worked out there.

There's a third stage. The poet is also a citizen and taxpayer, and
together with these particular aspects of that poem qua poem there
are also ways in which it is, in one form or another, a self-portrait.
And you can argue what the self-portraiture is. It doesn't
necessarily have to be the portrait of the individual; it can be, say
along Marxist lines, a self-portrait as the member of a class. There
are many ways that you can deal with the subject, but this is a viable method by which to proceed, and of course you may bring in
all a man's biographical details, his letters, and material like that.
Often some particular term in a poem will be clarified by something he said in a letter, just as Mr. Young was talking about some
of the stuff Ransom said in his poetry. He took letters that Ransom
had written to Tate. You can get a clearer example, but you have a
quite reasonable pattern there. There's no argument.

The only argument I found through my years of going about
criticism is that what you are confronted with—dealing with the
idea of my whole general subject—is the notion of symbolic action.[1] This is symbolic action: I'm talking, I'm using a symbol
system to you now—that's an example of symbolic action. The
term also moves into psychoanalytic lines the way that Freud uses
it. Let us say somebody can't make a decision, can't walk across the
street, or something like that. The term has a ring but you can
explain the ring. You don't have to have a term that stays put, as in
a dictionary: you just tell how it gets transformed under different
conditions. I can talk about symbolic action in terms of the way the
symbols are used in an individual poem, as though I didn't know

[1] *The Philosophy of Literary Form: Studies in Symbolic Action* (Baton Rouge:
Louisiana State University Press, 1941), pp. 8–18 and passim.

the author of it; or I can talk about symbolic action in general. What I found in my career, going about the country and talking to this group and that, is that when you talk about the poem individually you run across a lot of people in the audience who want you to talk about symbolic action in general. When you talk about symbolic action in general, they want you to talk about some particular poem individually. That part of it you can't resolve, but at least you can see the procedure that's operating there. You've got a perfectly good arrangement to work with.

Let me give you a little further example of how that general picture operates. If you start looking at dance, it is a symbol system; painting is a symbol system; and so forth. This doesn't just apply to the language; it happens that language is our department. Since our particular field is language, I stress that aspect of it fundamentally. If you look at the whole subject from the standpoint of symbolic action, here's the way it sets up: I have found that approaching things this way you have to throw out the aesthetic. I have to deal in the old scholastic line of rhetoric and poetic and dialectic. I'm not trying to fight with someone who wants to start with the aesthetic. All I'm saying is that so far as I can see this is the most direct way in which I can approach the analysis of a text. I am the kind of animal which is characterized by its special aptitude—not only aptitude but need—for symbolic action. I have to learn an arbitrary conventional symbol system in order to be considered a complete human being. Otherwise I'm a wolf child if I haven't learned some tribal language of some sort or other. Being this kind of animal, I want to exercise my resources of symbolic action—that is, symbolic action in and for itself—and simply to use the resources of the medium. It's the same as a bird flies or a fish swims, not always flying to get something or swimming to get something; but that's the kind of animal it is; or it's the kind of animal which is characterized by this aptitude and need involved in this matter of symbolic action. Therefore symbolic action that exercises that resource in and for itself is in the realm of poetics.

If, on the other hand, I use symbolic action to induce you to a response outside the work—I want you to vote for this person, or to buy this product, or to join this cause, or a sermon asking you to be good, behavior like that—this is rhetoric. That's the inducement to action, using symbolic action to induce a practical response outside the work. If I use the resource of symbolic action to discuss first principles, that's philosophy. If I use symbolic action to impart information, that's science. You see I don't have any problems here about which one is up and which is down. Now, if I want to talk about just the way the whole thing is put together, if I want to analyze which terms are high-level terms and which terms are low-level terms—that's what I would call dialectic. Socrates said that a good dialectician knows how to carve an idea to joints, and that's your fundamental picture of the field from this angle.

You see all of these battles just don't seem to exist because all these functions, every one of them, has its place in the stream of symbolic action. A lot of the battles don't exist in this method. I can say that a particular kind of scientific symbolic action leads to a certain kind of applied science and technology which happens to involve, say, unintended by-products like pollution. That's part of the structure and you don't have any difficulties. If I want to say that even the simple *use* of symbolic action in and for itself changes over the years as a result of differences in the social structure, I haven't insulted poetry. What happens is that as different systems develop—as you go from feudalism to capitalism—you run across corresponding changes in attitude, and of course the poet exploits those attitudes. You respond, you make those attitudes effective in and for themselves because you believe this or that.

I have a little idea about Shakespeare that doesn't fit the whole pattern, but it helps give the idea of what I have in mind. Suppose Shakespeare came from some other planet and learned English overnight, and the next day he said to somebody, "Say, what do these damn fools believe here? As soon as you tell me what they believe I'll write you a good tragedy or a good drama using those beliefs. I will turn those beliefs into a source of internal activity, an incitement." Of course that wouldn't have solved the whole problem because he had to have the experience with how birds sing, and things like that—all kinds of other things that wouldn't fit the pattern. But fundamentally you see the way in which a feudal structure is moving toward the business world, and he's right in the middle, and you can see the way he uses the different kinds of nomenclature that have to do with that. One of the fundamental ones is—I think one of the great test-words is—your attitude toward the ideal of ambition. You see, in the feudal system ambition was a very bad word and Shakespeare uses ambition that way. It still has that old quality. If you can imagine someone in a feudal system, if we had a psychology at that time, he'd go to a doctor, and say, "Doctor, what can you do with me? I'm just eaten up with ambition. How can we tone this down?" *Now* what can you do with me? I don't have enough ambition. So you find that kind of thing every

once in a while. You get a basic word which you can almost pin the
whole culture down to. Given a certain set of connotations around
a word, you can build up a structure of what poetic affections for
himself would allow the poet to use that particular attitude toward
that term.[2] So you build your recipes.

In this way I can use Aristotle's rhetoric, which is not usually related to the poetics. I can use the rhetoric as a perfect example of
how you can transform it for purposes of poetics. He tells you how.
If you want to build up a character to make him admirable, here's
the thing to say. If you want to smear him, here are the things to
say. He tells you how to persuade and dissuade. *"Laus et
vituperatio"*—praise and blame. Using that same kind of formula,[3]
instead of just having a person say these things, I can have him do
corresponding things and get my character built up that way. I can
have him both say and do. Therefore you get the fact that Shakespeare doesn't just build a character by what he says but also by his
relation to the action, by how he responds to the action.

That's your fundamental pattern, and I think if you start with
this notion of poetics and rhetoric, you've got the way right into
the whole subject. It got lost when that notion was thrown out and
we got aesthetics as the main term. As for the whole notion about
the ambiguity of words, their various meanings, if that issue came
up I would say that what actually happens with words is this: that
words have a double nature in this sense—that is, take the definition of a word just as it is in the dictionary—the word is just treated
in itself. It so happens that the word rhymes with some other word
or fits in a tonal relationship to some other word. This concept
came up very much in relation to Hopkins. That quality of the
word is not in the word itself. It happens by accident that these
words sound like other words. And this particular accident of words
makes sympathetic vibration possible. When you say one word
you've got these other terms vibrating in sympathy with it, and a
poet can bring out that quality, as Hopkins does. In its lexical
meaning the sound of a word doesn't have anything to do with it,
except to distinguish it from some other word. But once you use it
in poetry you've got this other quality since poetry is basically
sound. I don't think that poetry is for the eye in our tradition. If it's
real poetry, it has to be heard, either heard actually or heard in the

[2] In this connection see William Empson, *The Structure of Complex Words*
(New York: New Directions, 1951).

[3] *A Rhetoric of Motives* (1950; rpt. Berkeley and Los Angeles: University of
California Press, 1969), p. 299.

imagination. Of course when you say one word you can hear another, or else the poet can help you hear another by the way he brings those connections together.

I thought that Mr. Miller's discussion of Hopkins was absolutely superb, an engrossing treatment of literary developments. I think it's one of the most gratifying talks I ever heard, the way he carries that whole thing through. But because of his approach there was one thing left out. The essay was a discussion of "The Wreck of the Deutschland," and where was the wreck? He had everything but the wreck. I told that to a present member of the audience—and he said, "Oh, you mean like a discussion of *Hamlet,* without Hamlet?" It isn't quite as bad as that. But actually Hopkins was the wreck, and Hopkins was, not by tests I might have but by his own test, a very conscientious, guilty person. He just didn't sit and make out these little designs with words; he was working out the whole problem of the sacrifice that was involved.[4] Mr. Miller talked about the kind of terms that turned up in relation to grace. For example grace equals orgy, it equals eating, it equals being eaten. Those are particularly unusual words to equate with grace. Mr. Miller was really dealing with what I'm talking about, the implicit equations in the work. And I think when you work with terms like that, you find that you really are in this realm of personality.

This brings out the whole issue in which a lot of my colleagues are now interested—that of the marvels of verbal structure. But I have to push back now; they've brought that out too much. People have accused me of just reducing things to words; the whole system is absolutely the opposite of that. That is, I make a fundamental distinction. The verbal is what I call symbolic action, using symbol systems. The fundamental distinction is between action and motion. Motion is completely outside the realm of action. If you destroyed the whole human race, which is the typical symbol-using animal, the realm of motion would go right on. From the standpoint of symbolism, symbolic action, the ocean can equal mother, can equal death. You have all kinds of meanings. The ocean in the realm of mere motion is just exactly those tides and movements in the physical realm. I don't by any means want to be reductive—after all, if I called man the symbol-using animal, his animality is in the realm of motion. It's not in the realm of action. On the other hand you cannot use symbolic action without involving motion; that is, the very fact of my using symbolic action now

[4] For J. Hillis Miller's response see note 6 to "The Linguistic Moment in 'The Wreck of the Deutschland.' "

involves motions of this sort. It involves motions in my brain, it involves motions in your brain, it involves motions of the sounds going from me to you. The realm is very clear there. It's clear at that
extreme. I admit there are places where it gets mixed up. I think,
for instance, psychogenic illness is an example of where the realms
overlap. A mere set of irritations—say to do with your ambitions,
your appetites and so on—if they're not working right—can give
you peptic ulcers. The whole thing is built on a set of symbolism
and your identifications along that line, but the peptic ulcers are
actually in the realm of motion—your body. This will turn up when
I get to the difference between theology and logology.

I use theology as a basis for analogies to logologies—that is how
words about God would analogically be understood as words about
words.[5] I'm dealing with this realm of motion in its own terms, and
it is outside the realm of symbolic action. I take Aquinas's notion of
matter as the principle of individuation. I've run across this often in
talks. I was on a panel once with some sociologists, and practically
the whole group was talking about the fact that man is the social
animal and that therefore we're all part of the whole scheme and
so on. Nothing of the sort is true. The analogous principle to that in
the field of logology is this notion of the centrality of the nervous
system. In the realm of motion I live and die when my heart stops.
In the realm of symbolic action I can identify myself with this
cause, with this family, with this church, with this movement.
That's in the realm of symbolic action, but in the realm of motion
my appetites are my own. My pleasures and pains are my own. You
may sympathize with them, but I feel them immediately. This principle of the centrality of the nervous system is purely in the realm
of motion. But given this kind of animal with this aptitude and
necessity to learn symbol systems, then this centrality of the
nervous system can move you into the whole realm of symbolic action.

What I want to deal with next is an example of this principle of
logology in those lines that Mr. Cohen read from Milton. The fundamental point about those lines, from my point of view, is this:
the logology notices that the basic structure is yes and no, acceptance and rejection. Carrying that into the realm of the afterlife,
the ones who say yes to God's commands are in heaven; the ones
who say no to God's commands are going to rot in hell. Once you

[5] See *The Rhetoric of Religion: Studies in Logology* (Boston: Beacon Press,
1961).

see that, the whole fundamental nature of this concept finally gets down to this: is it yes or is it no? Then you understand why—I don't give a damn what the conventions are—you understand "*Nor* did they not perceive the evil plight / In which they were, or the fierce pains *not* feel; / Yet to their General's voice they soon obey'd / *In*numerable." The whole negative comes out because hell is the place of the greatest Faust; for example Mephisto stands for this principle of negation.

There's a lot more that I would like to say about that, but it would take too long. I want to plead for these three kinds of form which, I claim, cover the ground. I wrote this fifty years ago. I feel sort of ashamed of myself to go back to it, but nobody's paid any attention to it and I'd like the proper chance. There are three and only three principles of form fundamentally. The first is progressive form—from this, to this, to this: the pointing of the arrows. You lead the audience to expect certain elements. This is all built on the theory of expectation. The writer leads the audience to expect certain things and fulfills those expectations, and that's form. This principle of progressive form is basic. Then there's repetitive form. Repetitive form is any way in which the work goes on being itself. If it's all, say, in heroic couplets, all right, that's your repetitive form. Or insofar as a character, whatever he does, continues to act in character, that's repetitive form. You find that in very many ways Aristotle represents it in the *Poetics* where he says, "If a man is inconsistent he must be consistently so." It's the most beautiful example of that principle. It's a perfect example of repetitive form. Then Mr. Cohen brought out the third principle. (This is all developed in "Lexicon Rhetoricae" in my first book of criticism, *Counterstatement*).[6] He brings out *conventional* form. Each time you read a particular kind of literary form you have specific expectations. For instance in tragedy, you start out expecting someone to be sacrificed. You lead toward the fulfilling of that expectation. I think the simplest example of progressive form, and the one that keeps gnawing all the time, is poetic justice. It comes out where we resist it in the farthest ranges, for it still goes on completely, say, in comedy, where the likable people win and the dislikable people outwit themselves in the end. You get fundamental structure there.

[6]"*Form* in literature is an arousing and fulfilment of desires. A work has form in so far as one part of it leads a reader to anticipate another part, to be gratified by the sequence" (*Counterstatement* [New York: Harcourt, Brace, 1931], p. 157; see esp. pp. 157–64.)

This involves both progressive form and repetitive form. You have these developments carried out according to your recipe.

I want to talk about the further developments of this kind of form. I have to handle it in modern art, where you have to deal with that same principle in reverse. In other words you have these expectations, but you can also get effects by violating those expectations. I don't ask that everybody stick with the expectations as in the classical canon, but I would note them. I'd use those as my bench mark and then note them: what kinds of effects do I get by breaking them, or fragmenting them, and so on? I have an analysis of Ionesco's *Victims of Duty* which is based precisely on that principle. The play depends upon a whole set of fragmenting of the classical principle. For instance what Ionesco does is have the characters about every two minutes change their identity. But during that time they act in character, in that mood. Therefore they still have exactly the fundamental logic of the classical form, but they've done this trick with it. I could go on with that mode in itself; it's a marvelous set of tricks that the playwright uses.

From the standpoint of conventional form I am interested in the notion that there's only one further aspect of form—the repetitive and progressive—with regard to such media as drama, story, lyric, and music, and in all its traditional variants—namely conventional form. I label this aspect of form categorical expectancy. That is, you have an expectation before you even come to the play. For instance, there is the whole neoclassical notion of what a tragedy was as treated in France, by which Shakespeare was a barbarian because he violated the categorical expectations. He didn't come to a tragedy by starting out with a group of witches on the stage in *Macbeth*. He violated the form that fit; the whole form was based on types of solemnity. It wouldn't fit the scheme. So you have this sort of thing going on all the time. Incidentally there's a word—I never got along too well with Croce, but I think he did have one good notion along that line—what he called a palimpsest. He says that a great deal of criticism in effect paints a new portrait on top of an old one, because the critics don't know exactly how a word was used in the time when it appeared in a particular play, Palimpsest. So there is a sense in which you do have to have historical recovery in places where the nature of your terms or the nature of your forms gets lost, and here we return to Mr. Cohen. I don't think fundamentally that fact brings up any problem. You've made a mistake and someone can set you straight, and that's about all it amounts to, it seems to me.

Now I take some examples offered at random: the invocation to the muses, the theophany in a play of Euripides, the processional and recessional of an Episcopalian choir, the ensemble before the drop at the close of a burlesque show, the exordium in Greek-Roman oratory, the Sapphic ode, the triolet. Poets who begin beginnings *as* beginnings and endings *as* endings show the appeal of conventional form. Thus, in Milton's "Lycidas" we start distinctly with a sense of introduction—"Yet once more, O ye laurels, and once more"—and the form is brought to its dexterous, delightful close by the stanza, clearly an ending: "And now the Sun had stretch'd out all the hills, / And now was dropt into the Western bay." The whole thing is a beautiful example of the categorical expectation which you bring to the poem. You bring this love of beginning as beginning and ending as ending.

One thing that I will do, if I may, is to bring out the fact that what happens with this whole notion of form when you begin to look at this idea of categorical expectations. Shakespeare, for example, sets it up so that at the end of the first act he tells you exactly what's going to happen. In about two or three minutes of a Shakespearean play you know the situation, and what he does is to carry out the implications of that situation. You know right at the start—Lear doesn't but you do—that Cordelia's the good girl and Regan and Goneril are awful. He makes it that clear; he always makes the audience know exactly what the situation is. The people who don't know are the people on the stage. I think the whole notion of surprise has lost its point because now it seems that the surprise is in surprising the *audience*. The real thing is to surprise the people on the stage. In *Oedipus Rex* the surprise is Oedipus. (In the first place everybody knew the myth—the myth won't change—that he knew before the play started; and even if he didn't know the myth, within five minutes he knew that Oedipus was looking for himself and didn't know it.) Looking at things from this standpoint, that's where surprise actually lies, because otherwise how could you read the same play over and over again if it was based on surprising you, the audience? Obviously it wouldn't work. Your fundamental structure lies in the fulfillment of expectation.

What happened about the time of Ibsen was that the author, instead of starting out and telling you what the situation is and then developing the implications of it, presented a play in which the whole action is gradually releasing the information. You don't know what the whole situation is until the play is over. And then the next stage is represented by Pirandello. At the end the play-wright has transformed the action to the point where the audience has gone through this fog about what to expect. And then you get to Beckett! And the most marvelous thing is that if from this point of view you translate this thing in terms of, instead of *waiting* for Godot, you are *expecting* Godot (which is what the action in-volves), then you realize he has done the final trick. Now you don't ask that the modern playwright obey this original principle. This does not involve your dictating to the poet, the way third-rate critics dictated to first-rate poets when they used Aristotle, which I'm sure the critic himself wouldn't have done. If Aristotle were dealing with, say, a play like *The Death of a Salesman*, I think he would have made a new set of canons for that kind of a play, instead of asking whether it obeys the rules of classical Greek Athenian tragedy.

So there's the fundamental picture. You can use these basic prin-ciples of form—progressive, repetitive, and conventional—and I claim they cover the ground. (I claim the whole stress upon art types has just gone too far.) What I'm trying to do is like the old battle between the Platonist and the Aristotelian. The word I want to bring out is *entelechy*—that is, to analyze a work not from the standpoint that it represents some archetype coming from a path, but in the sense that it brings something to fulfillment. The en-telechy is a completion, a fulfilling of possibility.